About Me!
Sobre Mí!

S0-DMY-069

Hey!
Paste your picture here!

Write your name.

_____

_____

Age?

Date

_____

Greatness!
In this oval, write something that is great about you!

_____

_____

_____

Where do you live?
Your city _____
Your state _____

Top 5 Vacation Spots
List the top 5 places that you would like to visit.

_____

_____

_____

_____

_____

Who is your best friend?
My best friend is:

_____

Welcome to *Bridges*, where building partnerships between home and school is an important part of ensuring that all children perform at their true academic potential.

Bridges is a unique workbook series developed by classroom teachers and based on national standards in language arts and mathematics. *Bridges* workbooks (available for students in grade/skill levels Pre-K–Grade 5-6) review basic skills in reading, writing, math, and language arts from the grade students are leaving and preview upcoming skills to help prepare students for the grade ahead.

Bridges begins with a pre-assessment test module to help determine student skill level and a parents' guide to help parents become more involved with their children's education. The parents' guide provides tips and on how to encourage interest in reading and a "Blueprint" for success that discusses how to use the workbook most effectively.

Bridges is divided into three sections that progress in difficulty. Each section begins with an incentive contract calendar to help generate excitement and interest in completing assignments and to give parents and teachers a tool to gauge progress. Exercises are typically in half-page increments to give students with shorter attention spans or those who do not yet have a full mastery of the English language a variety of skills and manageable assignments. Exercise instructions are presented in English and Spanish to allow Spanish-speaking parents to become more involved with their children's assignments and overall education.

A post-assessment module is also included to help evaluate student progress. Each *Bridges* workbook includes a certificate of completion that can be awarded by a teacher or parent to recognize and reinforce the student achievement.

We wish you, and your child or students, success this year.

Level Blue = Transition from Grade 1 to 2

All rights reserved.
Copyright 1998, 2004 Federal Education Publishing

Reproduction in any manner, in whole or in part, in English or in other languages,
or otherwise without written permission of the publisher is prohibited.

For information, write: Bridges • PO Box 57936 • Salt Lake City, Utah 84157-0936 • 801-313-0332

Please visit our website at **www.BridgesProgram.com** for supplements, additions, and corrections to this book.

Second Edition 2004
Printed in the United States of America

ISBN: 1-932210-62-8

PRINTED IN THE UNITED STATES OF AMERICA
10 9 8 7 6 5 4 3 2

Table of Contents

Parents' Guide

"Getting the Most from Bridges"

You are the most important teacher your child will ever have. *Bridges* is a guided daily workbook to help you succeed in this role.

Studies indicate that basic learning skills are more easily acquired early in life, and small successes can have a lifelong effect on a child's accomplishments. In fact, the more often you tell your children they are intelligent, the more likely they are to become just that. Chances to make such comments present themselves every day, especially during summer or off-track breaks.

You can encourage your children's intellectual development by involving them in things you do. When you cook, point out what ingredients you use and what effect they have on the meal—you've taught vocabulary and science. Take time to explain the newscast—you've taught social studies. Take your child shopping and point out price, brand, and weight differences—you've taught math, economics, and consumer skills.

Of course, you can also encourage your children to learn by getting directly involved in their schoolwork with a book like *Bridges.* This workbook contains:

- Over <u>200 specially designed, self-motivating activities</u> to keep your child busy, happy, and learning. Each day includes an activity in reading, writing, arithmetic, and language. There are forty-five days in all.
- A <u>Parents' Guide</u> containing ideas for getting the most out of *Bridges.*
- A carefully selected <u>book list</u> full of works children love to read.
- An <u>Incentive Contract</u> to motivate and reward your child's efforts.
- "<u>Try Something New</u>" lists of creative ideas for when your child says, "What can I do? I'm bored."
- <u>High-Frequency Word Lists</u> with vocabulary to sound out, read, and spell.
- A frameable <u>Official Certificate</u> for successfully completing the workbook activities.
- A Spanish <u>Glossary</u> of terms used in the book. (Glossary words are marked with a ‡.)
- <u>Instructions</u> translated into Spanish to help you help your child.

Bridges is packed with ideas for extracurricular activities, as well as fun and challenging math, reading, writing, spelling, and identification exercises that will take your children a step ahead and <u>help them reach for the stars.</u>

Bridges Blueprint for Success

Summer Reading

- There is a suggested reading list on pages xxvi–xxvii.
- Experts recommend that you read to your pre-kindergarten through first grade children 5–10 minutes each day and ask questions about the story. For older children, the recommended daily reading times are—

  Grades 1–2, 10–20 minutes; Grades 2–3, 20–30 minutes; Grades 3–4, 30–45 minutes; Grades 4–5, 45–60 minutes; and Grades 5–6, 45–60 minutes.
- You and your child should decide the length of reading time and fill it in on the Incentive Contract Calendar.

Incentive Contract Calendar

- An Incentive Calendar is located at the beginning of each section.
- You and your child should sign an agreement for an incentive or reward before your child begins each section.
- When your child completes one day of *Bridges,* he/she colors or initials the ☆ (star).
- When your child completes the agreed reading time each day, he/she colors or initials the 📖 (book).
- Let your child explore and experiment with the "Try Something New" activities lists.

Sections of Bridges

- There are three sections in *Bridges.*
- Each section becomes progressively more challenging.
- There are four activities each day.
- Your child will need a pencil, eraser, ruler, and crayons to complete the activities.

Words to Sound Out, Read, and Spell

At the end of each book (except Pre-K and K-1) are lists of words to sound out, read, and spell. You can use these for a number of activities and word games you can play with your child:

- Choose your child's favorite words, make two sets of flash cards, and play the matching game (in order to keep the two matching cards, you have to know the word's meaning or spelling).
- Draw pictures of exciting words.
- Use as many words as you can from the list to make up five questions, statements, or explanations.
- Write a story using as many words as you can from the word list.
- Write a list of words you have a hard time spelling.
- Write a list of action verbs.
- Close your eyes, try to remember as many words as you can from the word list, and write them down.
- Practice writing each word five times.
- Write a list of words you find while traveling to the mountains, on vacation, or on the way to a friend's house.

10 Hints on How to Maximize *Bridges*

 Let your child explore the book by flipping through the pages and looking at the activities.

 Help select a good time for reading or working on the activities. Suggest a time before your child has played outside and becomes too tired to do his or her work.

 Provide any necessary materials. A pencil, ruler, eraser, and crayons are all that are required.

 Offer positive guidance. Children need a great deal of guidance. Remember, the activities are not meant to be tests. You want to create a relaxed and positive attitude toward learning. Work through at least one example on each page with your child. "Think aloud" and show your child how to solve problems.

 Give your child plenty of time to think. You may be surprised by how much children can do on their own.

 Stretch your child's thinking beyond the page. If you are reading a storybook, you might ask, "What do you think will happen next?" or "What would you do if this happened to you?" Encourage your child to name objects that begin with certain letters, or count the number of items in your shopping cart. Also, children often enjoy making up their own stories with illustrations.

 Reread stories and occasionally flip through completed pages. Completed pages and books will be a source of pride to your child and will help show how much he/she accomplished over the summer.

 Read and work on activities while outside. Take the workbook out in the backyard, to the park, or to a family campout. It can be fun wherever you are!

 Encourage siblings, baby-sitters, and neighborhood children to help with reading and activities. Other children are often perfect for providing the one-on-one attention necessary to reinforce reading skills.

 Give plenty of approval! Stickers and stamps, or even a hand-drawn funny face are effective for recognizing a job well done. At the end of the summer, your child can feel proud of his/her accomplishments and will be eager for school to start.

Guía para los padres

"Obteniendo el mayor beneficio de Bridges"

Los padres son los maestros más importantes que los niños tendrán en su vida. *Bridges* ofrece un cuaderno guía de ejercicios diarios para que usted tenga éxito en este papel.

Hay estudios que indican que las habilidades básicas de aprendizaje se obtienen con mayor efectividad durante los años formativos de la persona. Los pequeños triunfos pueden producir efectos permanentes en los logros de los niños. Mientras más a menudo les diga usted a sus hijos que son inteligentes, mayores son las posibilidades de que se conviertan justamente en ello.

Las oportunidades para hacerles tales comentarios a sus hijos se presentan a diario, especialmente durante las vacaciones de verano o los descansos entre periodos de estudio.

Puede motivar el desarrollo intelectual de sus niños al permitirles participar en actividades que usted hace. Por ejemplo, muéstreles los ingredientes que use y enséñeles el efecto que tienen en las comidas y les habrá enseñado vocabulario y ciencias. Tome tiempo para explicarles las noticias y les habrá enseñado ciencias sociales. Lleve a sus hijos de compras y enséñeles sobre las diferencias de precios, marcas y medidas, y les habrá enseñado matemáticas, economía y habilidades del consumidor.

Este cuaderno de ejercicios contiene:

- Más de <u>200 actividades especialmente diseñadas</u> para incentivar a los niños a que se motiven a sí mismos y se mantengan ocupados y felices a medida de que aprenden. Esta guía está dividida en cuatro actividades diarias: lectura, escritura, aritmética y uso del idioma. La guía presenta un programa de 45 días; cada página con el número del día pertinente.
- Una <u>Guía para los padres</u> que contiene pautas útiles sobre cómo usar mejor el libro.
- Una <u>lista de libros</u> cuidadosamente seleccionados de obras que a los niños les encanta leer.
- Un <u>Contrato de Incentivo</u> para motivar y premiar los esfuerzos de los niños.
- Una lista de ideas creativas "<u>Trata Algo Nuevo</u>" para cuando los niños pregunten: "¿Qué puedo hacer?, estoy aburrido".
- <u>Listas de palabras</u>, con vocabulario para pronunciar, leer y escribir.
- Un <u>Certificado Oficial</u> para cuando el niño haya completado exitosamente todas las actividades del libro.
- Un <u>Glosario en español</u> de términos utilizados en el libro. (Las plalbras que se encuentran en el glosario están marcadas con una ‡).
- <u>Instrucciones</u> traducidas al español para ayudarlo a usted y a su niño.

Bridges contiene muchísimas ideas para actividades extracurriculares, así como también divertidos y desafiantes ejercicios de matemáticas, lectura, escritura, ortografía e identificación, que <u>harán progresar a su niño y lo ayudarán a obtener las estrellas.</u>

Bridges Blueprint para el éxito

Lectura para el verano

- En la página XXVI encontrará una lista de sugerencias para lectura.
- Los expertos recomiendan que se le lea al niño entre edad preescolar y 1er grado, por 5 a 10 minutos diarios y que se le haga preguntas acerca de la historia. Para niños de mayor edad se recomienda una lectura diaria de:
     Grados 1–2: 10–20 minutos; Grados 2–3: 20–30 minutos; Grados 3–4: 30–45 minutos
     Grados 4–5: 45–60 minutos; Grados 5–6: 45–60 minutos.
- Usted y su niño deberán pactar el tiempo que dedicarán a la lectura y completar el Calendario de Incentivo de Actividades.

Contrato de Incentivo

- Al principio de cada sección se encuentra un Contrato de Incentivo.
- Usted y su niño deberán firmar un acuerdo de incentivo o recompensa antes de que el niño comience cada sección.
- Cuando el niño complete un día de *Bridges*, coloreará o escribirá sus iniciales en la ☆ (estrella).
- Cuando su niño complete el tiempo diario de lectura pactado, coloreará o escribirá sus iniciales en el 📖 (libro).
- Deje que el niño explore y experimente la lista de actividades <u>Trata Algo Nuevo</u>.

Secciones de Bridges

- *Bridges* contiene 3 secciones.
- Cada sección se torna progresivamente más desafiante.
- Cada día consta de cuatro actividades.
- El niño necesitará un lápiz, una goma, y lápices de colores para completar las actividades.

Palabras para pronunciar, leer y deletrear

Después de la última sección figuran palabras para pronunciar, leer y deletrear. Usted puede utilizar estas palabras para muchas actividades y juegos de palabras que realice con su niño:

- Elija las palabras favoritas de su niño, prepare dos juegos de tarjetas y juegue al *Juego de la Memoria*. Ponga las tarjetas boca abajo y dé vuelta de a dos a la vez, tratando de recordar las coincidencias a medida que avance (para quedarse con las dos tarjetas que coinciden, se debe saber o el significado o cómo se escriben).
- Haga dibujos de las palabras interesantes.
- Utilice la mayor cantidad posible de palabras de la lista para inventar cinco preguntas, oraciones declarativas o explicaciones.
- Escriba una historia utilizando la mayor cantidad posible de palabras de la lista.
- Escriba una lista de las palabras que más le cuesta deletrear.
- Haga una lista de verbos activos.
- Cierre los ojos, trate de recordar la mayor cantidad posible de palabras de la lista y escríbalas.
- Escriba cada palabra cinco veces.
- Haga una lista de palabras que encuentre mientras viaja a las montañas, vacaciona o se dirige a la casa de un amigo.

10 sugerencias para obtener el mayor beneficio de *Bridges*

 Deje que su niño explore el libro, hojeando las páginas y mirando las actividades.

 Seleccione un buen momento para la lectura y la realización de actividades. Sugiera un momento luego de que su niño haya jugado al aire libre y antes de que se encuentre demasiado cansado.

 Facilite el material necesario, generalmente todo lo que necesitará será: un lápiz, una regla, una goma y lápices de colores.

 Ofrezca una guía positiva. Los niños necesitan guía permanente. Recuerde que las actividades no son exámenes. Cree una actitud relajada y positiva hacia el trabajo escolar. Realice con el niño por lo menos un ejemplo de cada página. "Piense en voz alta" y muéstrele al niño cómo resolver los problemas.

 Dele al niño mucho tiempo para pensar. Se sorprenderá de cuánto pueden realizar los niños por sí solos.

 Extienda el pensamiento del niño más allá de las actividades de la página. Si está leyendo una historia puede preguntarle: "¿Qué crees que sucederá ahora?" o "¿Qué harías si te sucediera a ti?" Incentive a su niño a nombrar objetos que comiencen con ciertas letras o a que cuente los objetos de su carrito de compras. Muchas veces los niños también disfrutan inventando sus propias historias con ilustraciones.

 De vez en cuando, revise páginas ya finalizadas. Las páginas ya terminadas y los libros ya leídos serán una fuente de orgullo para su niño y lo ayudarán a demostrar lo mucho que ha logrado a través de las semanas.

 Lea y realice las actividades al aire libre. Lleve el libro de actividades al aire libre al jardín, al parque o a un campamento. ¡Puede ser divertido!

 Incentive a los hermanos, niñeras y niños del vecindario a que ayuden a su niño en las actividades y la lectura. Muchas veces otros niños son perfectos para proporcionar la atención recíproca que necesitan los lectores principiantes.

 ¡Muestre aprobación! Las calcomanías, las etiquetas y hasta una cara divertida dibujada por usted son un reconocimiento efectivo de un trabajo realizado satisfactoriamente. Cuando su niño haya completado el libro, cuelgue el certificado de logro en un lugar donde todos puedan verlo.

Using the Spanish Instructions in *Bridges*

Basic instructions in Spanish for each activity are provided in red underneath the English instructions. These are to help you as a parent understand the overall nature of the assignment and what tasks your child is supposed to complete. On pages 101–104, *Bridges* also includes a Spanish glossary of grammatical and mathematical terms which may be unfamiliar. All words included in the glossary are marked with a ‡. For example, one instruction reads:

> **Write adjectives in the blanks.**
> **Escribe adjetivos‡ en los espacios en blanco.**

The ‡ tells you that you will find an explanation for the word *adjective* in the glossary:

> **Adjetivo** (adjective)—una palabra que califica a un sustantivo o pronombre. Los adjetivos pueden describir cuántos, de qué tipo o cuál. En la oración "El hombre delgado cepillaba tres perros con un peine azul", *tres*, *delgado* y *azul* son adjetivos.

Note: Once he or she is old enough, your child should read the complete instructions in English. The English paragraphs sometimes contain additional information your child will need to complete the assignment. While this may be challenging at first, it will help your child develop important educational skills. As children work to understand the English instructions, they will not only strengthen their English skills; they will also develop strategies for learning, such as using context clues, a dictionary to look up unfamiliar terms, and a glossary. These are skills all students need, regardless of their native language.

Uso de las instrucciones en español en *Bridges*

Debajo de las instrucciones en inglés para cada actividad, encontrará instrucciones básicas en español escritas en rojo. El objetivo de estas instrucciones es ayudarlo a usted, como padre, a comprender la naturaleza general del trabajo y las tareas que se supone su niño debe realizar. En las páginas 101–104, *Bridges* también incluye un glosario en español de términos gramaticales y matemáticos que podrían resultarle poco comunes. Todas las palabras incluidas en el glosario se encuentran marcadas con una ‡. Por ejemplo, una de las instrucciones dice:

> **Write adjectives in the blanks.**
> **Escribe adjetivos‡ en los espacios en blanco.**

El ‡ le indica que encontrará una explicación de la palabra adjetivo en el glosario:

> **Adjetivo** (adjective)—una palabra que califica a un sustantivo o pronombre. Los adjetivos pueden describir cuántos, de qué tipo o cuál. En la oración "El hombre delgado cepillaba tres perros con un peine azul", tres, delgado y azul son adjetivos.

Nota: Una vez que el niño tenga la edad apropiada, deberá leer las instrucciones solamente en inglés. Muchas veces los párrafos en inglés contienen información adicional que su niño necesitará para completar la tarea. Aunque al principio esto puede resultar un desafío, ayudará a que su niño desarrolle habilidades educativas importantes. Al mismo tiempo que los niños trabajan para comprender las instrucciones en inglés, no solamente refuerzan sus habilidades con respecto al idioma, sino que también desarrollan estrategias de aprendizaje, como por ejemplo, el uso de pistas de contexto, de un glosario y de un diccionario para buscar términos desconocidos. Estas son habilidades que todos los estudiantes necesitan, sin importar cuál sea su lengua nativa.

How to Encourage Children to Pick Up a Book and Read

You can help your child develop good reading habits. Most experts agree that reading with your child is the most important thing you can do. To choose a good book, use *Bridges*' book list.

Set aside time each day to read aloud to your child at bedtime or after lunch or dinner. Read some of the books you enjoyed when you were young.

Visit the library to find books that meet your child's specific interests. Ask a librarian which books are popular among children of your child's grade. Take advantage of storytelling activities at the library. Ask the librarian about other resources, such as stories on CDs, cassettes, videotapes, records, and even computers.

Encourage and provide a variety of reading materials. Help your child read house numbers, street signs, signs in store windows, and package labels. Encourage your child to tell stories using pictures.

Best of all, show your child you like to read. Sit down with a good book. After supper, share stories and ideas that might interest your child from the newspapers and magazines you're reading.

Cómo motivar a los niños para que escojan un libro y lo lean

Usted puede ayudar a su niño a desarrollar buenos hábitos de lectura. La mayoría de los expertos coincide en que leer con su niño es lo más importante que usted puede hacer. Para elegir un buen libro, utilice la lista de libros *Bridges*.

Reserve un momento del día para leerle en voz alta a su niño: a la hora de irse a dormir o luego del almuerzo o de la cena. Lea algunos de los libros que a usted le gustaban cuando era niño. Visite la biblioteca para encontrar libros que coincidan con los intereses específicos de su niño.

Pregúntele a un bibliotecario cuáles son los libros populares entre los niños del mismo grado. Aproveche las actividades de narración de cuentos en las bibliotecas. Pregúntele al bibliotecario acerca de otros recursos, como historias en casetes, cintas de video, discos y computadoras.

Fomente y proporcione gran variedad de material de lectura. Ayúdele a su niño a leer los números de las casas, los carteles de las calles, los carteles en los escaparates y las etiquetas de envoltorios. Incentive a su niño a relatar historias basándose en dibujos.

Pero, por sobre todo, demuéstrele al niño que a usted le gusta leer. Siéntese con un buen libro. Luego de la comida comparta las historias e ideas del periódico o revistas que usted lee que puedan interesarle al niño.

Assessment Tests

A Word about Assessment

The goal of the assessment test is to help you discover what skills your students have acquired and what skills they need to learn. You can use the pretest at the beginning of a new school year or during the course of the school year to give you an idea of where your students are in their development. The post-test can then be used as a follow-up. As you give the assessment, talk with your students about their thinking. Ask questions about the answers they give. If a student cannot complete the assessment, you can use the assessment as a teaching tool. Walk the student through the assessment, teaching as you go.

Keys to Positive Assessment

Your students will need the assessment page and a pencil.

Provide a quiet place free of clutter and distractions.

If parents are administering the test at home, suggest that they try answering questions with a question. For example:

Student: *"What is this word?"*

Parent: *"What letters do you see in the word?"* or *"What sound does each letter make?"*

Instruct parents to refrain from immediately correcting their child and to note skills that need to be taught or reinforced. They should have the child move on if he or she is having difficulty.

Assessment Tests

The assessment tests are divided into four parts:

Assessment 1 assesses reading ability on a word and sentence level.

Assessment 2 assesses language skills and the ability to recognize such things as compound words, contractions, base words, and verb tense.

Assessment 3 provides writing practice that also tests knowledge of parts of speech, basic grammar, and sentence logic.

Assessment 4 assesses beginning math skills including numeration, place value, greater and less than, time and money values, addition, subtraction, and word problems.

The *Bridges* Assessments Include three Parts:

1. An assessment to test what students already know.
2. A post-assessment to test what students have learned.
3. An assessment analysis to refer you to activity pages in *Bridges* where students can practice specific skills.

Assessment Test Analysis
Bridges 1–2

After you review your child's assessment test, match the problems that contain incorrect answers to the *Bridges* pages below. Pay special attention to these pages and ensure that your student receives supervision and extra help if needed. In this way, your child will strengthen skills in these areas.

Reading Skills

4, 6, 8, 9, 10, 12, 14, 16, 18, 21, 23, 30, 31, 32, 37, 42, 46, 48, 49, 51, 52, 56, 58, 62, 68, 70, 74, 86, 88, 90, 92, 96

Language Skills

Contractions:	15, 24, 26, 75, 81, 89
Compound Words:	28, 67
Base Words:	55
Verb Forms:	62, 76

Writing Skills

Proofreading:	22, 59, 71
Parts of Speech:	72, 92
Sentence Structure:	30, 44, 94
Punctuation:	10, 20, 76

Mathematics

Counting & Numeration:	3, 9, 13, 35, 37, 53, 55, 63, 71, 73, 95
Money:	11, 17, 19, 45, 57, 85
Time:	7, 39
Addition & Subtraction:	5, 21, 23, 25, 27, 29, 43, 49, 51, 59, 61, 69, 75, 77, 79, 83, 87, 89, 91, 93
Word Problems:	31, 41, 45, 57, 67
Fractions:	81

Read the sentences. Put the letter of the picture that goes with the sentence on the line.

1. _____The fan is very pretty.

2. _____The rock broke the glass.

3. _____The bird sat on the branch.

4. _____The ball was in the mitt.

5. _____The boy rode his bike.

6. _____The clock rang at two o'clock.

7. _____The cake had one candle.

8. _____The lamp fell off the table.

9. _____The cat went to sleep on the rug.

10. _____The mother bird fed her baby in the nest.

Circle the word that goes with the picture.

11. dim dime diem

12. hawk hake hauck

13. boyl boil bole

14. shell chell sell

15. storem sorm storm   

16. wale whale whail

Write the two words that make up each contraction.

1. isn't

2. couldn't

3. don't

4. I've

5. we're

Draw a line between the two little words that make up each compound word.

6. campfire

7. sunglasses

8. bathrobe

9. hairspray

10. cupcake

Write the base word.

11. skipped

12. baking

13. tallest

14. silliest

15. teaches

Write the past tense of each word.

16. run

17. hop

18. walk

19. chase

20. cry

Circle the mistakes in each sentence. Write the sentence correctly.

1. Is mr. white going to work today.

_____

_____

2. my big sister sed that i is a pest.

_____

_____

3. can I rid yur bike.

_____

_____

4. My Teacher Likes to red lots uf Book

_____

_____

5. watch out four that falling rock?

_____

_____

Circle the nouns (naming words) and underline the verbs (action words) in each sentence.

6. The children played at the park.

7. Mrs. Lopez whistled for her dog.

8. My friends watched the movie.

9. Mandy ate some watermelon.

10. The dog barked at the children.

Use the words to make a sentence.

11. plays My baseball brother.

_____

_____

12. the went zoo Our to class.

_____

_____

Write the missing number.

1. 46 _____ 48

2. 59 _____ 61

3. 70 _____ 72

4. 17 _____ 19

5. 2, 4, 6, _____ 10 _____ _____ 16 _____ 20

6. 30, 35, 40 _____ 50 _____ _____ 65 _____ 75

7. 10, 20, 30 _____ 50 _____ 70 _____ _____ 100

Write how many tens and how many ones.

8. 73 = _____ tens _____ ones

9. 40 = _____ tens _____ ones

10. 16 = _____ ten _____ ones

11. 29 = _____ tens _____ ones

Circle the larger number.

12. 34 or 43

13. 19 or 22

14. 24 or 21

15. 98 or 89

Count the money and write the amount.

16.

17.

18.

19.

Write the time shown on each clock.

20.

_____ : _____

21.

_____ : _____

22.

_____ : _____

Solve the problems.

23.
7	5	8	9	6
+ 5	+ 9	+ 7	+ 3	+ 8

24.
10	12	14	15	13
− 6	− 4	− 7	− 6	− 5

25.
4	5	6	7	9
4	2	3	4	7
+ 3	+ 6	+ 2	+ 3	+ 3

26.
23	34	81	63	25
+ 12	+ 24	+ 17	+ 26	+ 40

27.
68	39	77	87	46
− 25	− 17	− 41	− 30	− 24

28. Josh had 8 baseball cards. His brother had 9 baseball cards.
How many cards do the brothers have altogether? _____

29. Lindsey had 13 marbles. She lost 7 marbles.
How many marbles does she have now?_____

30. Mindy ate 3 cookies, Rachel ate 2 cookies, and Brock ate 4 cookies.
How many cookies did the children eat in all?_____

Read the sentences. Put the letter of the picture that goes with the sentence on the line.

1. _____The vet pet my dog.

2. _____The boy dug in the sand.

3. _____The dog just had a bath.

4. _____The mouse jumped out of the box.

5. _____The kids are washing the car.

6. _____A frog sat on a rock.

7. _____The boy caught a fish.

8. _____The girl has a letter and a bag.

9. _____The boy will help his mom cook.

10. _____The pot on top of the stove was hot.

Circle the word that goes with the picture.

11. cak cake cack

14. bell bill blell

12. yawn yane yarn

15. coren korn corn

13. coyn coin cone

16. pale pail pal

Write the two words that make up each contraction.

1. didn't
2. wouldn't
3. doesn't
4. you've
5. you're

Draw a line between the two little words that make up each compound word.

6. doghouse
7. baseball
8. sandcastle
9. sunshine
10. sailboat

Write the base word.

11. hopped
12. coming
13. prettiest
14. farmer
15. boxes

Write the past tense of each word.

16. laugh
17. giggle
18. sing
19. cry
20. sip

Circle the mistakes in each sentence. Write the sentence correctly.

1. Where is mrs. brown going.

2. yesterday i rided my bike to skool.

3. can I have sum of yur candy bar.

4. my big brother is in the sixth grad.

5. I likes to red lots uf book

Circle the nouns (naming words) and underline the verbs (action words) in each sentence.

6. The boys swam in the pool.

7. Our teacher wrote on the chalkboard.

8. My family plays baseball.

9. Rachel eats pancakes.

10. The cat sat on the big chair.

Use the words to make a sentence.

11. plays My the sister piano.

12. the went park My to family.

Write the missing number.

1. 37 _____ 39

2. 51 _____ 53

3. 79 _____ 81

4. 15 _____ 17

5. 22, 24, 26, _____ 30 _____ _____ 36 _____ 40

6. 20, 25, 30 _____ 40 _____ _____ 55 _____ 65

7. 10, 20 _____ _____ 50 _____ 70 _____ _____ 100

Write how many tens and how many ones.

8. 82 = _____ tens _____ ones

9. 30 = _____ tens _____ ones

10. 19 = _____ ten _____ ones

11. 51 = _____ tens _____ one

Circle the larger number.

12. 26 or 62

13. 18 or 17

14. 45 or 54

15. 99 or 89

Count the money and write the amount.

16.

17.

18.

19.

Write the time shown on each clock.

20.

_____ : _____

21.

_____ : _____

22.

_____ : _____

Solve the problems.

23.
$$
\begin{array}{r} 7 \\ +\,4 \\ \hline \end{array}
\qquad
\begin{array}{r} 6 \\ +\,9 \\ \hline \end{array}
\qquad
\begin{array}{r} 7 \\ +\,7 \\ \hline \end{array}
\qquad
\begin{array}{r} 8 \\ +\,9 \\ \hline \end{array}
\qquad
\begin{array}{r} 3 \\ +\,8 \\ \hline \end{array}
$$

24.
$$
\begin{array}{r} 10 \\ -\,4 \\ \hline \end{array}
\qquad
\begin{array}{r} 12 \\ -\,8 \\ \hline \end{array}
\qquad
\begin{array}{r} 14 \\ -\,6 \\ \hline \end{array}
\qquad
\begin{array}{r} 15 \\ -\,7 \\ \hline \end{array}
\qquad
\begin{array}{r} 13 \\ -\,6 \\ \hline \end{array}
$$

25.
$$
\begin{array}{r} 4 \\ 4 \\ +\,5 \\ \hline \end{array}
\qquad
\begin{array}{r} 1 \\ 7 \\ +\,6 \\ \hline \end{array}
\qquad
\begin{array}{r} 4 \\ 3 \\ +\,2 \\ \hline \end{array}
\qquad
\begin{array}{r} 7 \\ 4 \\ +\,5 \\ \hline \end{array}
\qquad
\begin{array}{r} 9 \\ 6 \\ +\,5 \\ \hline \end{array}
$$

26.
$$
\begin{array}{r} 20 \\ +\,17 \\ \hline \end{array}
\qquad
\begin{array}{r} 54 \\ +\,23 \\ \hline \end{array}
\qquad
\begin{array}{r} 71 \\ +\,17 \\ \hline \end{array}
\qquad
\begin{array}{r} 53 \\ +\,36 \\ \hline \end{array}
\qquad
\begin{array}{r} 27 \\ +\,30 \\ \hline \end{array}
$$

27.
$$
\begin{array}{r} 67 \\ -\,15 \\ \hline \end{array}
\qquad
\begin{array}{r} 47 \\ -\,22 \\ \hline \end{array}
\qquad
\begin{array}{r} 77 \\ -\,34 \\ \hline \end{array}
\qquad
\begin{array}{r} 96 \\ -\,41 \\ \hline \end{array}
\qquad
\begin{array}{r} 34 \\ -\,13 \\ \hline \end{array}
$$

28. Martin checked out 3 books about airplanes and 6 books about animals. How many books did Martin check out altogether? _____

29. Jared had 15 words on his spelling test. He misspelled 2 words. How many words did he spell correctly? _____

30. McKenzie bought 3 red balloons, 5 blue balloons and 7 yellow balloons. How many balloons did she buy all together? _____

Assessment 1 • Reading Skills

1. B
2. I
3. H
4. D
5. F
6. J
7. A
8. E
9. G
10. C

11. dime
12. hawk
13. boil
14. shell
15. storm
16. whale

Assessment 2 • Language Skills

1. is   not
2. could   not
3. do   not
4. I   have
5. we   are
6. camp / fire
7. sun / glasses
8. bath / robe
9. hair / spray
10. cup / cake

11. skip
12. bake
13. tall
14. silly
15. teach
16. ran
17. hopped
18. walked
19. chased
20. cried

Assessment 3 • Writing Skills

1. Is (mr) (white) going to work today(.)
   Is Mr. White going to work today?

2. (my) big sister (sed) that (i is) a pest.
   My big sister said that I am a pest.

3. (can) I (rid) (yur) bik(e.)
   Can I ride your bike?

4. My (Teacher) (Likes) to (red) lots (uf) (Book)
   My teacher likes to read lots of books.

5. (watch) out (four) that falling roc(k?)
   Watch out for that falling rock!

6. The (children) played at the (park)

7. (Mrs. Lopez) whistled for her (dog.)

8. My (friends) watched the (movie.)

9. (Mandy) ate some (watermelon.)

10. The (dog) barked at the (children.)

11. My brother plays baseball.

12. Our class went to the zoo.

Assessment 4 • Mathematics

1. 47
2. 60
3. 71
4. 18
5. 8   12   14   18
6. 45   55   60   70
7. 40   60   80   90

8. 7 tens 3 ones
9. 4 tens 0 ones
10. 1 ten 6 ones
11. 2 tens 9 ones

12. (43)
13. (22)
14. (24)
15. (98)

16. 50¢
17. 38¢
18. 37¢
19. 66¢

20. 7:30
21. 11:00
22. 2:30

23. 12   14   15   12   14
24. 4   8   7   9   8
25. 11   13   11   14   19
26. 35   58   98   89   65
27. 43   22   36   57   22

28. 17 baseball cards
29. 6 marbles
30. 9 cookies

Post-assessment 1 • Reading Skills

1. D
2. B
3. F
4. I
5. G

6. C
7. J
8. H
9. A
10. E

11. cake
12. yarn
13. coin

14. bell
15. corn
16. pail

Post-assessment 2 • Language Skills

1. did   not
2. would   not
3. does   not
4. you   have
5. you   are

6. dog / house
7. base / ball
8. sand / castle
9. sun / shine
10. sail / boat

11. hop
12. come
13. pretty
14. farm
15. box

16. laughed
17. giggled
18. sang
19. cried
20. sipped

Post-assessment 3 • Writing Skills

1. Where is (mrs.) (brown going.)
   Where is Mrs. Brown going?

2. (yesterday) (i) (rided) my bike to (skool.)
   Yesterday I rode my bike to school.

3. (can) I have (sum) of (yur) candy ba(r.)
   Can I have some of your candy bar?

4. (my) big brother is in the sixth (grad.)
   My big brother is in the sixth grade.

5. I (likes) to (red) lots (uf) boo(k)
   I like to read lots of books.

6. The (boys) swam in the (pool.)

7. Our (teacher) wrote on the (chalkboard.)

8. My (family) plays (baseball.)

9. (Rachel) eats (pancakes.)

10. The (cat) sat on the big (chair.)

11. My sister plays the piano.

12. My family went to the park.

Post-assessment 4 • Mathematics

1. 38
2. 52
3. 80
4. 16
5. 28   32   34   38
6. 35   45   50   60
7. 30   40   60   80   90

8. 8 tens 2 ones
9. 3 tens 0 ones
10. 1 ten 9 ones
11. 5 tens 1 one

12. (62)
13. (18)
14. (54)
15. (99)

16. 45¢
17. 31¢
18. 43¢
19. 71¢

20. 5:30
21. 2:00
22. 7:30

23. 11   15   14   17   11
24. 6   4   8   8   7
25. 13   14   9   16   20
26. 37   77   88   89   57
27. 52   25   43   55   21

28. 9 books
29. 13 words
30. 15 balloons

Reading Book List

Ackerman, Karen
Song and Dance Man

Ahlberg, Janet
Funnybones

Allard, Harry
Miss Nelson Is Missing!

**Andersen, Hans Christian
(retold by Anne Rockwell)**
The Emperor's New Clothes

Arnold, Tedd
No Jumping on the Bed!

Bemelmans, Ludwig
Madeline

Berenstain, Stan and Jan
The Berenstain Bears

Brown, Marcia
Stone Soup: An Old Tale

Capucilli, Alyssa Satin
Mrs. McTats and Her Houseful of Cats

Cerf, Bennett
Bennett Cerf's Book of Laughs
Bennett Cerf's Book of Riddles

Choi, Yangsook
The Name Jar

Cohen, Barbara
Molly's Pilgrim

Cosgrove, Stephen
Leo the Lop—I, II, III, IV
Hucklebug
Morgan and Me
Kartusch
Snaffles

Dicks, Terrance
Adventures of Goliath

Dorros, Arthur
Abuela

Duvoisin, Roger
Petunia
Veronica

Eastman, P. D.
Are You My Mother?
Go, Dog. Go!

Ehlert, Lois
Market Day

Freeman, Don
Corduroy

Grimm, Jacob
The Frog Prince

Hall, Donald
Ox-Cart Man

Hutchins, Pat
Don't Forget the Bacon!
Good-Night, Owl!
Rosie's Walk

Isadora, Rachel
My Ballet Class

Kellogg, Steven
Paul Bunyon, a Tall Tale

Leaf, Munro
The Story of Ferdinand
Wee Gillis

Lobel, Arnold
Frog and Toad series

McCaughrean, Geraldine
Saint George and the Dragon

McCloskey, Robert
Make Way for Ducklings

Minarik, Else Holmelund
Little Bear

O'Connor, Jane
The Teeny Tiny Woman

Park, Barbara
Junie B. Jones books

Peet, Bill
The Ant and the Elephant
Big Bad Bruce
Buford, the Little Bighorn
The Caboose Who Got Loose
Jethro and Joel Were a Troll

Rylant, Cynthia
Henry and Mudge books

Schwartz, Alvin
In a Dark, Dark Room

Sendak, Maurice
Higglety Pigglety Pop!
Where the Wild Things Are

Seuss, Dr.
The Cat in the Hat
Green Eggs and Ham
The Foot Book

Sharmat, Marjorie Weinman
Nate the Great and the Musical Note

Slobodkina, Esphyr
Caps for Sale

Steig, William
Gorky Rises

Steptoe, John
Mufaro's Beautiful Daughters

Thomas, Shelley Moore
Good Night, Good Knight

Viorst, Judith
Alexander and the Terrible, Horrible,
No Good, Very Bad Day

Waber, Bernard
Ira Sleeps Over

Ward, Lynd
The Biggest Bear

Yolen, Jane
Picnic with Piggins

© Federal Education Publishing   Level Blue

Ready for Reading

✔ Reading has been around for thousands of years and can open your mind to new ideas by making you think in different ways than television or radio!

✔ The more you read, the smarter you get!

Books I Have Finished Reading

Title	Author	Pages	Date Finished	Great	Evaluation Okay	Bad

Incentive Contract Calendar

Month (Mes) _____

My parents and I decided that if I complete 15 days of *Bridges*™ and read _____ minutes a day, my incentive/reward will be:

(Si yo completo 15 días de *Bridges*™ y leo _____ minutos al día, mi recompensa será:)

_____

Child's Signature (Firma del Niño)_____

Parent's Signature (Firma del Padre)_____

Day 1 (Día 1) ☆ 📖 _____

Day 2 ☆ 📖 _____

Day 3 ☆ 📖 _____

Day 4 ☆ 📖 _____

Day 5 ☆ 📖 _____

Day 6 ☆ 📖 _____

Day 7 ☆ 📖 _____

Day 8 ☆ 📖 _____

Day 9 ☆ 📖 _____

Day 10 ☆ 📖 _____

Day 11 ☆ 📖 _____

Day 12 ☆ 📖 _____

Day 13 ☆ 📖 _____

Day 14 ☆ 📖 _____

Day 15 ☆ 📖 _____

bridges

Parent: Initial the _____ for daily activities and reading your child completes.

Padre: (Marque _____ para las actividades y lectura que su niño complete.)

Child: Color the ☆ for daily activities completed.

Niño: (Colorea la ☆ para las actividades diarias que completes.)

Child: Color the 📖 for daily reading completed.

Niño: (Colorea el 📖 para las lecturas diarias que completes.)

Try Something New
Fun Activity Ideas

1 Sign up for summer classes at community education departments or local parks.
Inscríbete en lecciones de verano en los departamentos de educación de tu comunidad o en los parques locales.

2 Make a chart for summer chores with incentives.
Planifica tareas domésticas con incentivos para el verano.

3 Write to a relative about your summer plans.
Escríbele a un pariente sobre tus planes para el verano.

4 Check the library for free children's programs.
Infórmate en la biblioteca sobre programas gratuitos para niños.

5 Make labels for household objects to help practice reading.
Colócales etiquetas con el nombre a objetos de tu hogar para practicar lectura.

6 Start a journal of summer fun.
Comienza un diario del verano.

7 Zoo contest—find the most African animals.
Competencia en el zoológico: encuentra la mayor cantidad de animales africanos.

8 Shop together—use a calculator to compare prices per pound.
Haz las compras acompañado: usa una calculadora para comparar precio por libras.

9 Tune up your bike. Wash it, too.
Pon a punto tu bicicleta y lávala.

10 Arrange photo albums.
Ordena los álbumes de fotos.

11 Play flashlight tag.
Juega a la pesca de la luz.

12 Check out a science book and try some experiments.
Toma prestado de la biblioteca un libro de ciencias y haz algunos de los experimentos.

13 Make up a story at dinner. Have each person add a new paragraph.
Inventa una historia a la hora de la cena. Cada persona debe agregar un párrafo nuevo.

14 Learn about the summer solstice. Time the sunrise and sunset.
Aprende acerca del solsticio de verano. Toma la hora de la salida y de la puesta del sol.

15 Bubble fun: one-third cup liquid dishwashing soap, plus two quarts water. Use bent wire or pipe cleaners for dippers.
Diversión con burbujas: un tercio de taza de jabón lavavajilla más dos cuartos de agua. Usa un alambre doblado o un limpiador de cañerías como burbujero.

Write to 100.
Escribe hasta 100.

1	2			5					10
			14					19	
		23				27			
31				35					
	42						48		
					56				60
			64					69	
		73			76				
81									90
					96				

Circle the first letter underneath each picture if the picture begins with that sound. Circle the second letter if it ends with that sound. Color the pictures.

Encierra en un círculo la primera letra debajo del dibujo si éste comienza con ese sonido en inglés. Encierra en un círculo la segunda letra si el dibujo termina con ese sonido. Colorea los dibujos.

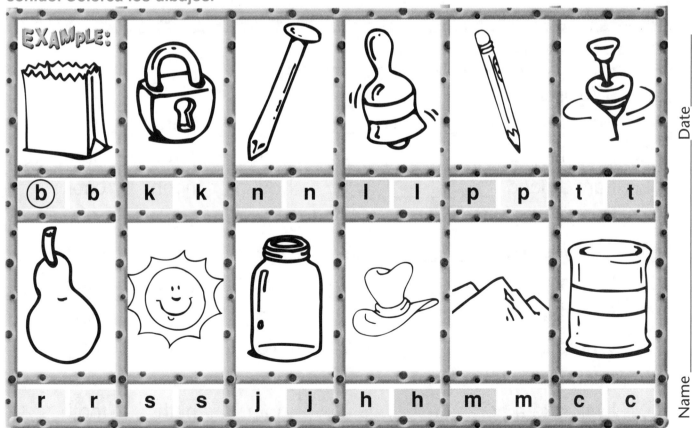

Date _____

Name _____

Write the capital letters of the alphabet.

Escribe el alfabeto en letra mayúscula.

EXAMPLE:

Circle and write the correct word.

Encierra en un círculo y escribe la palabra correcta.

EXAMPLE:

1.	We will go in the _____van_____.	van	can	ran
2.	I can help the _____.	mat	man	tan
3.	I am a good_____.	book	moon	cook
4.	He is in his _____.	red	bed	fan
5.	Can you get a _____?	the	it	book
6.	I am a _____man.	sad	glass	sled
7.	Find the big_____.	tug	pig	pink
8.	Where is the _____?	hid	run	flag
9.	I can run and _____.	jump	cup	went
10.	I will take a hot _____.	moth	bath	tooth

Add or subtract.
Suma o resta.

3	4	5	2	0	8	1	7
+2	+3	+0	+1	+1	+1	+5	+2

4	9	7	6	5	3	0	8
-2	-3	-7	-4	-1	-2	-0	-5

9	0	3	8	4	7	5	5
-4	+6	+5	+2	-3	-5	+5	-3

Circle the first letter in the box below each picture if the picture begins with that sound. Circle the second letter if the picture ends with that sound. Color the pictures.

Encierra en un círculo la primera letra debajo del dibujo si éste comienza con ese sonido en inglés. Encierra en un círculo la segunda letra si el dibujo termina con ese sonido. Colorea los dibujos.

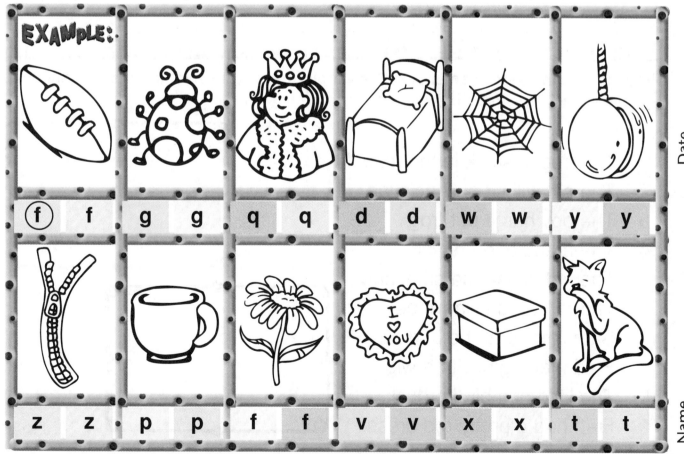

Write the lowercase letters of the alphabet.
Escribe el alfabeto en letra minúscula.

EXAMPLE:

Practice reading these sentences. Draw a picture of your two favorite sentences.
Lee estas oraciones. Haz dibujos de tus oraciones favoritas.

1. The dog is stuck in the mud.
2. The cat will sit on Ann's lap.
3. The boy has a pet frog.
4. The man sat on his hat.
5. The hat is flat and smashed.
6. The rat ran on Sam's bed.
7. Sam is mad at the bad rat.
8. Fred met a girl with a wig.
9. The little bug bit the duck.
10. Fran had a pretty red dress.

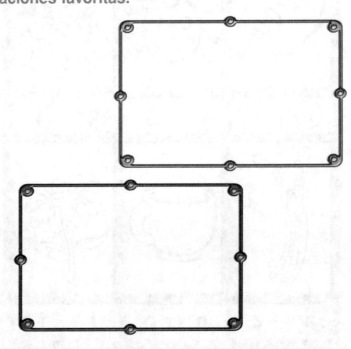

Write the correct time on the small clocks. Draw hands on the big clocks.

Escribe la hora correcta en los relojes pequeños. Dibuja manecillas en los relojes grandes.

9:00

_____:_____

7:00

_____:_____

3:00

_____:_____

Write the long vowel sound next to each picture. Color the picture.

Escribe el sonido de la vocal larga al lado de cada dibujo. Colorea el dibujo.

Date _____

Name _____

Match the sentence with the correct picture. Write the sentence number in the box.

Une la oración con el dibujo correcto. Escribe el número en el recuadro.

1. "Thank you for cleaning my yard!"
2. Dan and Trevor lick their ice cream.
3. The ice cream truck is coming.
4. The sun is very hot.

Draw and color pictures to go with these words.

Haz dibujos que coincidan con estas palabras.

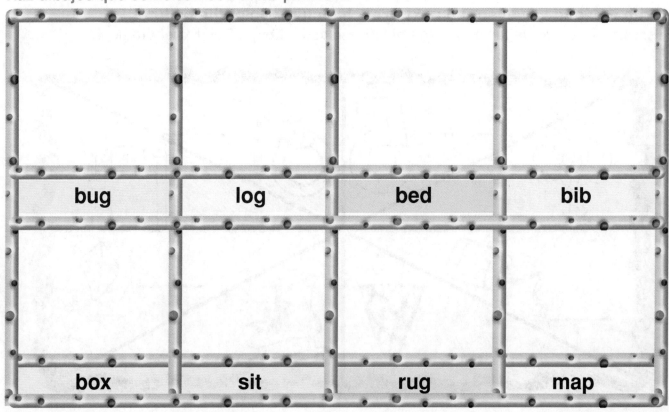

| bug | log | bed | bib |
| box | sit | rug | map |

Complete the counting pattern.
Completa el patrón de números.

1 2 ___ ___ 5 6 7 ___ ___ 10 ___ ___
13 14 ___ 16 ___ ___ 19 ___ 21 ___ ___ 24 ___

31 ___ ___ 34 ___ ___ 36 ___ ___ ___ 40 41 ___ ___ ___
44 ___ ___ 47 ___ ___ 50 ___ ___ 53 ___ ___ ___

___ ___ 77 78 ___ ___ ___ 82 ___ 84 ___ ___ 87
88 ___ ___ ___ 92 ___ ___ ___ 96 ___ ___ ___ 100

Long and Short Vowels. Circle the correct word and color the picture.
Encierra la palabra correcta en un círculo y colorea el dibujo.

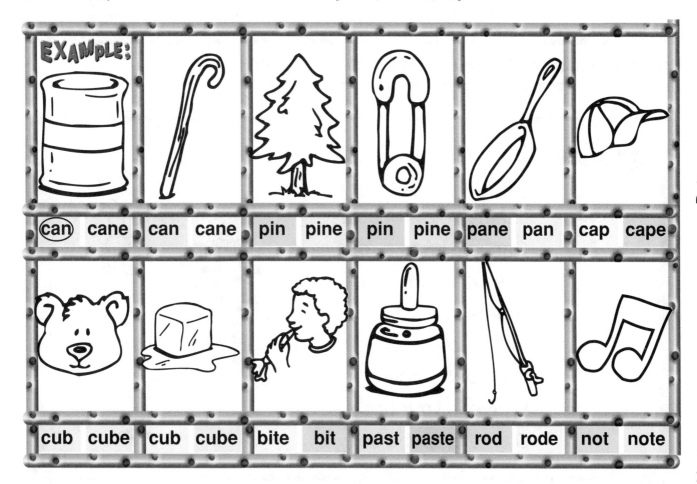

EXAMPLE:					
(can) cane	can cane	pin pine	pin pine	pane pan	cap cape
cub cube	cub cube	bite bit	past paste	rod rode	not note

© Federal Education Publishing 9 Level Blue

Name ___ Date ___

Practice writing your first and last name.
Practica escribir tu nombre y tu apellido.

End each sentence with the correct punctuation mark: (.), (!), or (?).
Termina cada oración con el signo de puntuación correcto: (.), (!) o (?).

EXAMPLE: Is your pet fat__?__

Do you like gum____

Jan can blow bubbles____

Can you jump a rope____

The woman was mad____

Are bears fuzzy____

Babies cry a lot____

Are clouds white____

Where is your nose____

Did he drop the box____

Count the money and write in the amount.
Cuenta el dinero y escribe la cantidad.

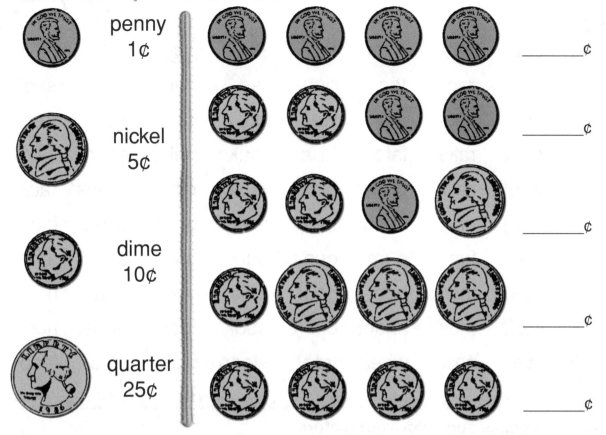

penny 1¢

nickel 5¢

dime 10¢

quarter 25¢

Color the short vowel pictures blue and the long vowel pictures green.
Colorea de azul los dibujos con vocales breves‡ y de verde los dibujos con vocales largas.

© Federal Education Publishing

11

Level Blue

Name _____

Date _____

Circle words that rhyme with the first word.
Encierra en un círculo las palabras que riman con la primera palabra.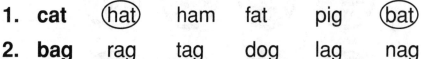

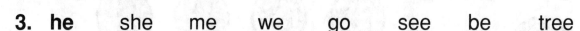

EXAMPLE:

1.	**cat**	(hat)	ham	fat	pig	(bat)	(rat)	(sat)
2.	**bag**	rag	tag	dog	lag	nag	big	sag
3.	**he**	she	me	we	go	see	be	tree
4.	**cake**	rake	late	lake	make	bake	stake	said
5.	**bank**	sank	drank	pink	sunk	tank	prank	rack
6.	**sing**	ring	song	thing	wing	bring	sting	big
7.	**run**	fun	gum	gun	sun	bun	spun	tin
8.	**coat**	moon	boat	goat	joke	shout	float	moat
9.	**look**	took	shoot	book	cook	rock	boost	hook
10.	**seat**	neat	wheat	treat	sleep	beat	sled	leap

Follow these directions and color your picture.
Sigue estas instrucciones y colorea tu dibujo.

1. Draw a tree.
2. Put a bird in your tree.
3. Draw a flower.
4. Draw a boy and his dog.
5. Draw a girl on a rock.
6. Give your picture a title.

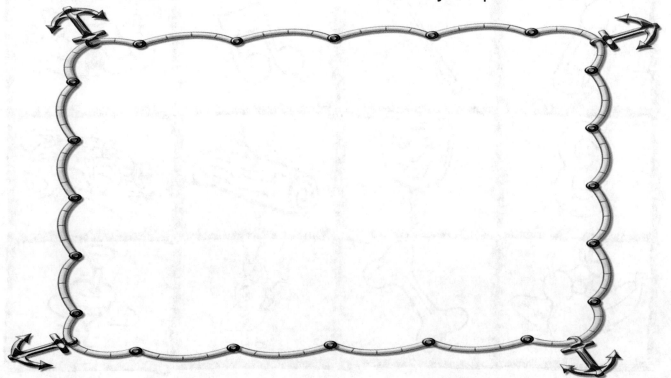

Count tens and ones.
Cuenta decenas y unidades.

EXAMPLE:

 ___24___

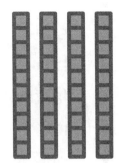 _____

 _____

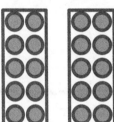 _____

_____

_____

  _____

  _____

Write the short vowel below the picture.
Escribe la vocal breve‡ debajo del dibujo.

EXAMPLE:

o
___

_____

_____

_____

_____

_____

_____

Date _____

Name _____

Draw a line between the opposites.
Une con una línea los opuestos.

EXAMPLE:

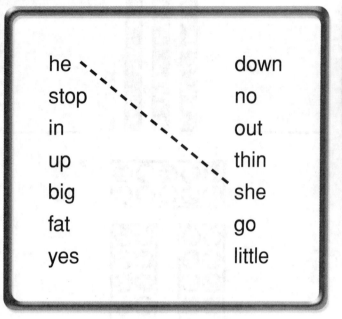

he	down
stop	no
in	out
up	thin
big	she
fat	go
yes	little

soft	clean
hot	slow
fast	cold
left	hard
off	bottom
dirty	right
top	on

Circle yes or no. Draw a picture of your favorite sentence.
Encierra en un círculo yes o no. Haz un dibujo de tu oración favorita.

1. Can a car jump?   yes   (no)
2. Can a rug be wet?   yes   no
3. Can men skip?   yes   no
4. Is a kitten a baby cat? yes   no
5. Do fish have fins?   yes   no
6. Can feet hop and run?   yes   no
7. Do rocks need sleep?   yes   no
8. Can hats fly?   yes   no
9. Do cows give milk?   yes   no
10. Can a leg be sore?   yes   no
11. Can a baby cry?   yes   no
12. Can a boy sing?   yes   no
13. Can a bear swim?   yes   no
14. Can a cow eat a lot?   yes   no

Read and answer these math problems.
Lee y resuelve estos problemas de matemáticas.

1. Griffin has two green cars and eight red cars in his train. How many cars does Griffin have in all?

_____ green cars   _____ red cars   _____ cars in train

2. There were five birds in one nest. Then two birds flew away. How many birds were left in the nest?

_____ – _____ = _____

3. Matt had nine spelling words. He missed two words. How many words did he get right?

$9 - 2 =$ _____

For each set of words, write the contraction in the word blank.
Escribe la contracción en el espacio en blanco.

EXAMPLE:

1. it is

2. you will

3. I am

4. we will

5. they have

6. he will

we'll   ~~It's~~   you'll   I'm   he'll   they've

Date _____

Name _____

Draw a picture the color of the word.

Haz un dibujo del color de la palabra.

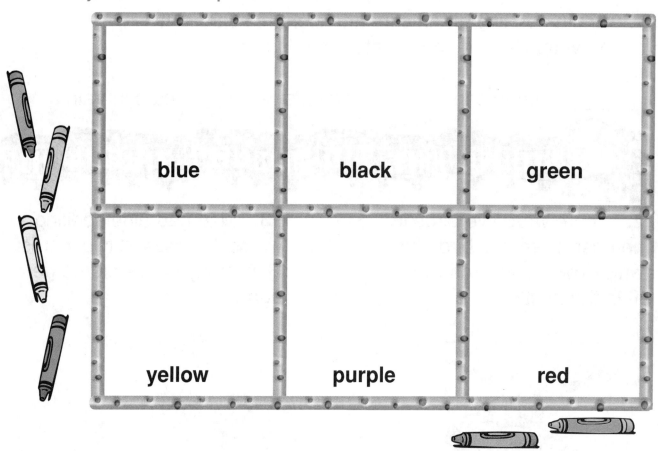

| blue | black | green |
| yellow | purple | red |

Circle the right word.

Encierra en un círculo la palabra correcta.

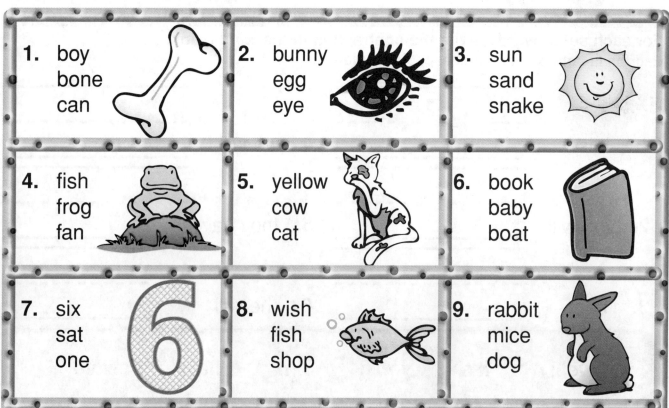

1. boy
   bone
   can

2. bunny
   egg
   eye

3. sun
   sand
   snake

4. fish
   frog
   fan

5. yellow
   cow
   cat

6. book
   baby
   boat

7. six
   sat
   one

8. wish
   fish
   shop

9. rabbit
   mice
   dog

Count the money and write in the amount.
Cuenta el dinero y escribe la cantidad.

EXAMPLE:

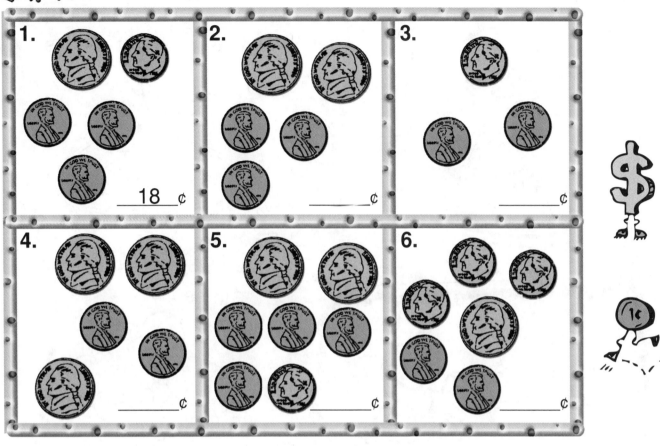

1. _____18_____ ¢

2. _____ ¢

3. _____ ¢

4. _____ ¢

5. _____ ¢

6. _____ ¢

Write and finish this sentence in three different ways.
Escribe y termina esta oración de tres formas distintas.

"I like my class because..."

1.

2.

3.

Date_____

Name

In each sentence, draw a circle around the two words that rhyme.
En cada oración, encierra en un círculo las dos palabras que riman.
Color the picture.
Colorea el dibujo.

1. The fish is in a dish.

2. The man in the boat is wearing a coat.

3. There is a bug in my mug.

4. The bee is in the tree.

Put the words in alphabetical order.
Escribe las palabras en orden alfabético.

apple	1. _____		dog	1. _____
cat	2. _____		fish	2. _____
book	3. _____		elephant	3. _____
girl	1. _____		lamp	1. _____
ice	2. _____		king	2. _____
hat	3. _____		map	3. _____
hot	1. _____		well	1. _____
sit	2. _____		sleep	2. _____
cry	3. _____		dark	3. _____

Match the price of each toy with the correct amount of money.
Une el precio de cada juguete con la cantidad de dinero correcta.

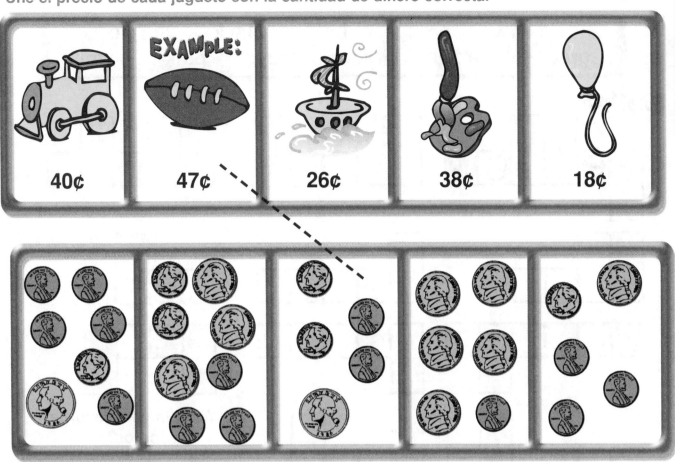

40¢   EXAMPLE: 47¢   26¢   38¢   18¢

Find and circle the words.
Encuentra y encierra en un círculo las palabras.

EXAMPLE:

I	F	L	Y	P	B	M	Y	W	C
D	C	C	M	I	D	T	A	I	L
E	F	E	H	E	I	I	G	L	I
H	I	G	H	G	M	E	U	D	M
N	I	G	H	T	E	I	Y	A	B

ice   wild   my   fly

pie   high   guy   dime

night   climb   tie   tail

Date

Name

Write the color words that fit in the boxes.
Escribe los nombres de los colores en los recuadros que corresponde.

| yellow | orange | blue | black | purple |
| green | brown | red | gray | pink | white |

EXAMPLE:

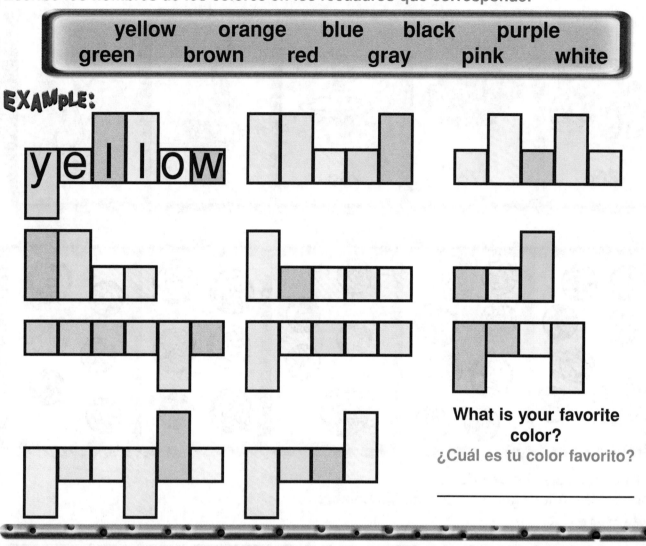

y e l l o w

What is your favorite color?
¿Cuál es tu color favorito?

_____

Put a (.) or a (?) at the end of each sentence. Draw a picture of your favorite sentence.
Coloca un (.) o un (?) al final de cada oración. Haz un dibujo de tu oración favorita.

1. The dog ran down the road_____
2. Do you like to play football_____
3. Can a cat jump over a ditch_____
4. We are going to school today_____
5. What time do you go to bed_____
6. Is green the color of a frog_____
7. The farmer has ten horses_____
8. Ann has a new blue dress_____
9. We will walk to the store_____
10. Will your mom go swimming with us_____

Add or subtract.

Suma o resta.

5 + 6 = _____   6 + 4 = _____   3 + 8 = _____

7 + 3 = _____   9 - 5 = _____   6 - 4 = _____

10 + 1 = _____   8 - 3 = _____   2 + 9 = _____

8 - 2 = _____   10 - 4 = _____   9 - 3 = _____

10 - 5 = _____   8 + 2 = _____   9 + 3 = _____

6 + 5 = _____   7 + 4 = _____   8 + 0 = _____

Match each sentence with the correct job title.

Une cada oración con el nombre del oficio correcto.

EXAMPLE:

I like to fish. - - - - - - - - - - - - -   farmer

I deliver many things near and far.   pilot

I can stop traffic with one hand.   truck driver

I grow things to eat.   fisherman

I fly airplanes.   baker

I bake cakes and cookies.   police officer

Date

Name

© Federal Education Publishing   21   Level Blue

Find the hidden picture. Color the long i (ī) words blue and the short i (ĭ) words green. (The sound of (ī) can be in words with the letter y, too.)
Colorea las palabras con i larga‡ (i) de azul y las palabras con i breve‡ (i) de verde.

bib	fry	tie	light	my	sigh	try	wig
six	bike	sign	pie	guy	by	high	if
fib	gift	pit	dry	bite	miss	fish	lit
chin	sit	pill	time	night	hid	bill	quit
bin	mit	tin	cry	dime	win	fit	will
pin	fine	lie	sight	why	right	shy	fin
zip	ride	buy	side	hike	kite	nine	did

Something is wrong with one word in each sentence. Find the word and correct it!
En cada oración hay una palabra con un error. Corrígela.

1. Emily bocked a cake.

2. Ashley and i went to the zoo.

3. grant has a train.

4. Clean your toy rom.

5. Dan will ride hiz bike.

Complete the number families.
Completa las familias de números.

2 + 3 = ☐   7 + 2 = ☐   5 + 3 = ☐

3 + ☐ = 5   ☐ + 7 = 9   ☐ + ☐ = 8

5 - 2 = ☐   9 - ☐ = 2   8 - ☐ = ☐

☐ - 3 = 2   9 - ☐ = 7   ☐ - 3 = ☐

Circle the largest number in each set.
Encierra en un círculo el número mayor de cada serie.

17 or 71   91 or 19   67 or 72

34 or 30   26 or 41   29 or 40

Read each puzzle. On the line, write a word that rhymes with the underlined word.
Lee cada acertijo. Escribe una palabra que rime con la palabra subrayada.

1. It rhymes with <u>mat</u>.
It is a good pet.
It is a

_____

- - - - - - - - - - - - -

_____

2. It rhymes with <u>boys</u>.
Kids love to play with
them. They are

_____

- - - - - - - - - - - - - -

_____

Date

Name

Match the word pairs to the right contraction.
Une los pares de palabras con la contracción adecuada.

EXAMPLE:

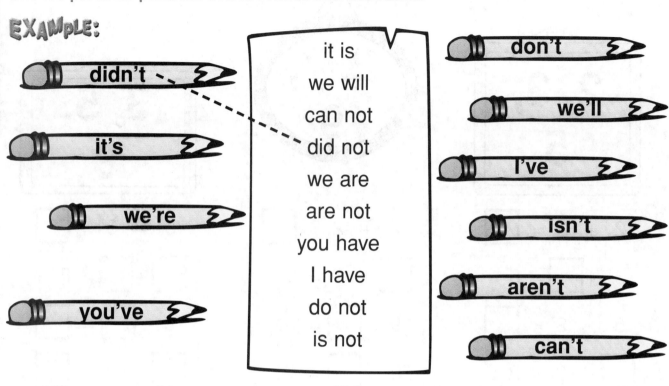

it is
we will
can not
did not
we are
are not
you have
I have
do not
is not

didn't

it's

we're

you've

don't

we'll

I've

isn't

aren't

can't

Unscramble the sentences.
Ordena las oraciones.

1. swim like Ducks to.

2. pigs mud Do play in the?

3. nests Birds in trees make.

4. fun today Are having you?

Add or subtract.
Suma o resta.

8 + 2 = _____	10 - 4 = _____	2 + 1 = _____
4 + 4 = _____	5 - 2 = _____	7 - 3 = _____
3 + 7 = _____	6 - 3 = _____	5 - 4 = _____
1 + 9 = _____	4 - 4 = _____	10 - 5 = _____
3 + 3 = _____	7 - 4 = _____	3 + 2 = _____
6 + 4 = _____	3 - 1 = _____	5 + 4 = _____
5 + 2 = _____	9 - 4 = _____	6 - 2 = _____
10 + 0 = _____	8 - 3 = _____	4 + 4 = _____

Blends are two different consonants which join together to make a certain sound. Write the blends for the pictures below.
Escribe los grupos consonánticos de los dibujos a continuación.

EXAMPLE:

d r _____ _____ _____ _____ _____ _____

_____ _____ _____ _____ _____ _____ _____ _____

Date _____

Name _____

Match the contractions with the word pairs. Write the answer on the line.

Une las contracciones con los pares de palabras. Escribe la respuesta en la línea.

has   not

could   not

isn't
couldn't
hasn't
can't

can   not

is   not

fuel   rub   huge   trunk

tube

cube

snug

Read the word on each balloon. If the word has a long u (ū) sound, color the balloon yellow. If the word doesn't have a long u (ū) sound, color the balloon any color but yellow.

Si la palabra contiene el sonido de u larga (ū), colorea el globo de amarillo. Si no, colorea el globo de cualquier otro color.

Circle each problem that equals the number at the start of each row.

Encierra en un círculo todos los problemas que tengan por resultado el número al comienzo de cada línea.

EXAMPLE:

7	(3 + 4)	(9 - 2)	(5 + 2)	7 - 2	6 - 4	(7 + 0)	(8 - 1)
5	6 - 1	0 + 5	4 + 1	9 - 4	10 - 5	8 + 2	7 - 2
4	3 + 1	5 - 2	6 + 3	10 - 6	9 - 5	2 + 2	8 - 4
8	10 - 2	2 + 6	9 - 1	8 - 0	3 + 5	7 + 2	1 + 7
3	5 - 4	2 + 1	6 - 3	9 - 6	0 + 3	9 - 2	7 - 4
6	12 - 6	6 + 5	5 + 1	10 - 4	8 - 3	4 + 2	7 - 1

Find and circle the following words:

Encuentra y encierra en un círculo estas palabras:

boy	bay	enjoy	say
joy	hay	toy	day

d	f	b	o	y	b	h	g	e
a	l	e	d	c	p	a	h	n
y	m	k	b	q	r	y	i	j
o	n	q	a	t	t	s	j	o
r	s	a	y	j	o	y	v	y
s	w	x	u	c	y	f	g	z

Date

Name

Combine the word and the picture to form a compound word. Write it in the blank.

Combina la palabra y el dibujo para formar una palabra compuesta.

EXAMPLE:

1. cook   +   =   ___cookbook___

2. base   +   =   _____

3.    +   bell   =   _____

4. life   +      =   _____

5.    +   fighter   =   _____

6. cat   +      =   _____

Put a 1, 2, or 3 in each box to show the right order.

Coloca 1, 2 o 3 en cada recuadro para indicar el orden correcto.

☐ Emily ran into a rock with her bike.

☐ Emily and her bike tipped over.

☐ Emily went for a bike ride.

☐ Tim woke up and got out of bed.

☐ Tim rode the bus to school.

☐ Tim ate a big breakfast.

Complete the number families.
Completa las familias de números.

4, 9, 5

6, 2, 8

3, 7, 10

4 + 5 = ____

5 + 4 = ____

9 - 5 = ____

9 - 4 = ____

6 + ____ = 8

2 + ____ = ____

8 - ____ = 2

8 - ____ = ____

____ + ____ = ____

____ + ____ = ____

____ - ____ = ____

____ - ____ = ____

Write the beginning and ending sounds.
Escribe los sonidos iniciales y finales.

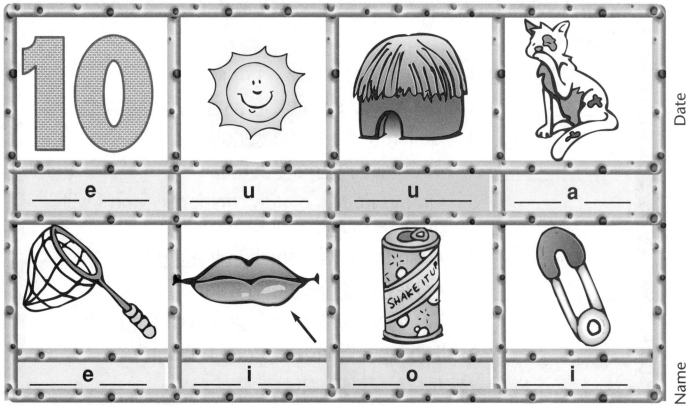

____ e ____

____ u ____

____ u ____

____ a ____

____ e ____

____ i ____

____ o ____

____ i ____

© Federal Education Publishing

29

Level Blue

Date

Name

Circle the sentence that goes with the picture.
Encierra en un círculo la oración que coincide con el dibujo.

1. Emily walked up the stairs.

2. Emily walked down the stairs.

3. Emily sat on the stairs.

1. Bob threw the baseball to his dad.

2. Bob threw the baseball to Ashley.

3. Bob threw the baseball to his mom.

Are the underlined words telling <u>who</u>, <u>what</u>, <u>when</u>, or <u>where</u>? Write the answer at the beginning of each sentence.
¿Las palabras subrayadas indican quién, qué, cuándo o dónde? Escribe la respuesta en el espacio en blanco.

EXAMPLE:

who

1. <u>My mother</u> is going home.

2. We will go swimming <u>tomorrow morning</u>.

3. Children like to eat <u>candy</u>.

4. The ball is <u>under the bed</u>.

5. On the <u>Fourth of July</u>, my family and I will go on a picnic.

6. A big truck was stuck <u>in the mud</u>.

7. <u>Ashley and her friend</u> went on a trip.

8. The boy lost his <u>new skates</u> at the park.

9. <u>The clown</u> made everyone laugh.

Read and answer the math problems below. Write each problem.
Lee y resuelve estos problemas matemáticos. Escribe cada problema.

1. The elves made four shoes the first night and six shoes the second night. How many shoes did they make?

_____ + _____ = _____

2. Tim had three balls. He found three more. How many balls does he have in all?

_____ + _____ = _____

3. A farmer had nine cows. He sold five of them. How many cows does he have left?

_____ - _____ = _____

Write the correct color words.
Escribe los colores correctos.

Snow is _____.

Grapes are _____.

The lettuce is _____.

The sun is _____.

My hat is _____.

Sam's dog is _____.

My friend's house is _____.

Tomatoes are _____.

Chocolate candy is _____.

Marshmallows are _____.

Teddy bears are _____.

The sky is _____.

Trees are _____.

My shoes are _____.

My eyes are _____.

My hair is _____.

Mud is _____.

Goldfish are _____.

Blackboards are _____.

Dad's car is _____.

Date _____

Name _____

Find and circle the words with the long u vowel sound (ū).

Encuentra y encierra en un círculo las palabras con el sonido de la vocal larga u (ū).

use	huge	glue	music
cube	cute	salute	tune

g	l	u	e	l	s	q	t	m
c	a	s	f	r	a	b	u	u
u	o	e	h	t	l	m	n	s
t	d	n	c	h	u	g	e	i
e	j	s	u	k	t	p	v	c
i	w	c	u	b	e	x	e	g

Check the box which best describes the picture.

Marca el recuadro que mejor describe el dibujo.

☐ The mouse is in the box.

☐ The mouse is under the box.

☐ The mouse jumped out of the box.

☐ The bird is sleeping.

☐ The bird loves to sing.

☐ The bird never sings.

Incentive Contract Calendar

Month (Mes) _____

My parents and I decided that if I complete 15 days of *Bridges*™ and read _____ minutes a day, my incentive/reward will be:

(Si yo completo 15 días de *Bridges*™ y leo _____ minutos al día, mi recompensa será:)

_____

Child's Signature (Firma del Niño)_____

Parent's Signature (Firma del Padre)_____

Day 1 (Día 1) ☆ 📖 _____

Day 2 ☆ 📖 _____

Day 3 ☆ 📖 _____

Day 4 ☆ 📖 _____

Day 5 ☆ 📖 _____

Day 6 ☆ 📖 _____

Day 7 ☆ 📖 _____

Day 8 ☆ 📖 _____

Day 9 ☆ 📖 _____

Day 10 ☆ 📖 _____

Day 11 ☆ 📖 _____

Day 12 ☆ 📖 _____

Day 13 ☆ 📖 _____

Day 14 ☆ 📖 _____

Day 15 ☆ 📖 _____

bridges

Parent: Initial the ____ for daily activities and reading your child completes.

Padre: (Marque ____ para las actividades y lectura que su niño complete.)

Child: Color the ☆ for daily activities completed.

Niño: (Colorea la ☆ para las actividades diarias que completes.)

Child: Color the 📖 for daily reading completed.

Niño: (Colorea el 📖 para las lecturas diarias que completes.)

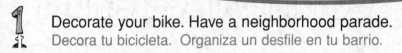

Try Something New
Fun Activity Ideas

1 Decorate your bike. Have a neighborhood parade.
Decora tu bicicleta. Organiza un desfile en tu barrio.

2 Get the neighborhood together and play hide-and-seek.
Reúne a los vecinos y juega a las escondidas.

3 Take a tour of the local hospital.
Ve de una visita al hospital local.

4 Check on how your garden is doing.
Revisa en qué estado está tu jardín.

5 Make snow cones with crushed ice and punch.
Haz conos de nieve con hielo picado y ponche.

6 Go on a bike ride.
Participa en un paseo en bicicleta.

7 Run through the sprinklers.
Corre a través de las regaderas.

8 Create a family symphony with bottles, pans, and rubber bands.
Crea una sinfónica familiar con botellas, cacerolas y ligas.

9 Collect sticks and mud. Build a bird's nest.
Junta palitos y barro. Construye un nido de pájaros.

10 Help plan your family grocery list.
Ayuda a planificar la lista de comestibles de tu familia.

11 Go swimming with a friend.
Ve a nadar con un amigo.

12 Clean your bedroom and closet.
Limpia tu habitación y tu ropero.

13 Go to the local zoo.
Visita el zoológico local.

14 In the early morning, listen to the birds sing.
Escucha a los pájaros cantar temprano a la mañana.

15 Make a cereal treat.
Organiza un banquete de cereales.

Complete the counting patterns.
Completa las series.

10	20		40			70			100

5	10	15			35	40		
55			70			90		

2	4		8		12			18		22
	26			32				42		

Write in the short and long vowels.
Escribe las vocales breves‡ y largas.

EXAMPLE:

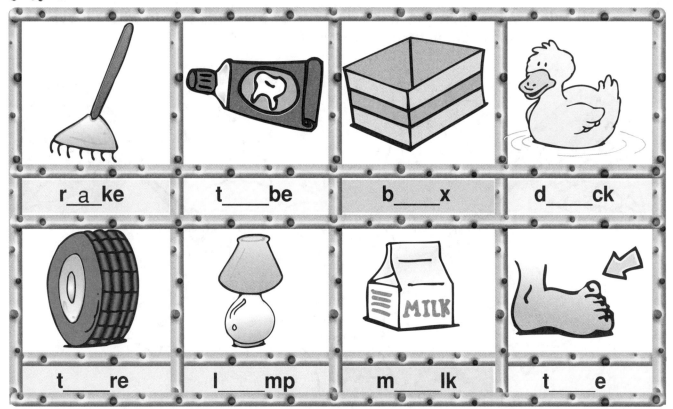

r_a_ke	t___be	b___x	d___ck

t___re	l___mp	m___lk	t___e

© Federal Education Publishing   35   Level Blue

Name _____   Date _____

A hobby is something we enjoy doing in our spare time. Some children like to make things. Some like to collect things. Some play music, and some children do other things. Hobbies are fun. Do you have a hobby?

Draw and color a picture of one of your hobbies!
Haz y colorea un dibujo de uno de tus pasatiempos.

Catch each butterfly. Put each one in the right net by drawing a line to where it belongs.
Dibuja una línea desde cada mariposa hasta la red correcta.

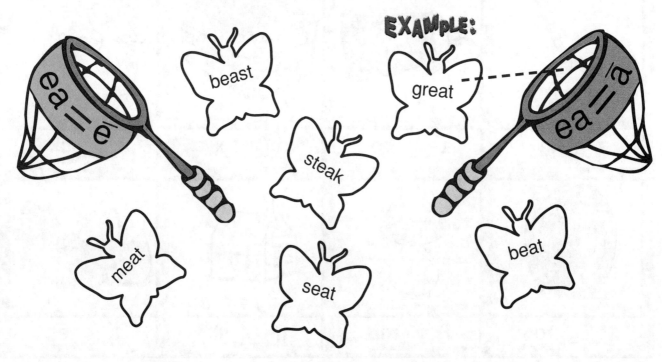

EXAMPLE:

beast

ea = ē

great

ea = ā

steak

meat

seat

beat

Decide how many tens and how many ones make up each number.
Decide cuántas decenas y cuántas centenas forman cada número.

EXAMPLE:

26 = __2__ tens __6__ ones   41 = _____ ones _____ tens

45 = _____ tens _____ ones   69 = _____ ones _____ tens

65 = _____ ones _____ tens   84 = _____ tens _____ ones

17 = _____ ones _____ tens   72 = _____ ones _____ tens

50 = _____ tens _____ ones   39 = _____ tens _____ ones

97 = _____ ones _____ tens   51 = _____ ones _____ tens

35 = _____ tens _____ ones   100 = _____ tens _____ ones

Read the sentence; then follow the directions.
Lee la oración y luego sigue las indicaciones.

Ashley hugged her dog three times.

1. Circle the word <u>hugged</u>.
2. Draw a box around the word that tells who Ashley hugged.
3. Underline the word that tells who hugged the dog.
4. Draw a picture of Ashley and her dog.

Date

Name

Number these sentences in the order they happened.
Enumera estas oraciones en el orden en que sucedieron.

- [ ] The sun came out. It was a pretty day.
- [ ] The thunder roared, and the lightning flashed.
- [ ] It rained and rained.
- [ ] Emily put her umbrella away.
- [ ] Emily walked under her umbrella.
- [ ] The clouds came, and the sky was dark.

Finish the story.
Termina la historia.

Once there was a sun. The happy sun loved to shine its bright rays onto the earth because...

Draw the hands to match the time, or write the time to match the hands.

Dibuja las manecillas para que coincidan con la hora, o escribe la hora para que coincida con las manecillas.

2:30   ____:____   ____:____   11:00

____:____   10:30   5:00   7:30

Circle the letters that spell the beginning sound of each picture.

Encierra en un círculo las letras que muestren el sonido inicial de cada dibujo.

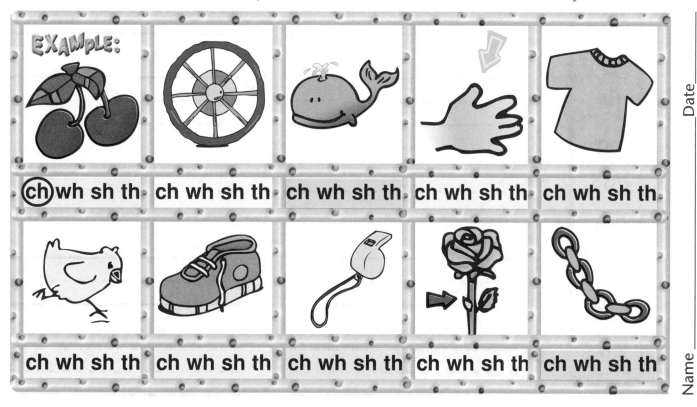

EXAMPLE:
(ch) wh sh th   ch wh sh th   ch wh sh th   ch wh sh th   ch wh sh th

ch wh sh th   ch wh sh th   ch wh sh th   ch wh sh th   ch wh sh th

© Federal Education Publishing   39   Level Blue

Read and decide.

Lee y decide qué encontró el hombre.

One day, a man went on a hunt. He hunted for a long time. At the end of the day, he was very happy. What do you think the man found? Did he find something to eat? Did he find something pretty? Did he find something funny? Decide what the man found and draw a picture of it!

Put the following words in alphabetical order.

Escribe las siguientes palabras en orden alfabético.

he	
up	
fat	
little	
big	
stop	
and	
out	
slow	
go	

1. _____   6. _____

2. _____   7. _____

3. _____   8. _____

4. _____   9. _____

5. _____   10. _____

Solve these problems.
Resuelve estos problemas.

1. Dan found five bees.
   Ashley found five bees.
   How many bees are there
   in all?

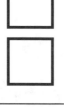

+

_____ bees

2. Lisa has four fish.
   Mike has six fish.
   How many fish are
   there in all?

+

_____ fish

**Word Study
and
Spelling List**

dime	make
name	plate
gave	size
nine	five
lake	bake
time	wise

Write the words with the long <u>a</u> (ā) sound.
Escribe estas palabras con el sonido <u>a</u> largo (ā).

_____ _____ _____

_____ _____ _____

Write the words with the long <u>i</u> (ī) sound.
Escribe estas palabras con el sonido <u>i</u> largo (ī).

_____ _____ _____

_____ _____ _____

Date

Name

Read each story. Choose the best title.
Lee las historias. Elige el mejor título.

Travis is up now. He hits the ball. "Run, Travis, run! Run to first base, then to second. Can you run to home base?"

1. Running
2. Travis Plays
3. Travis's Baseball Game

A rabbit can jump. Frogs can jump, too—but a kangaroo is the best jumper of all!

1. Jumping Rabbits
2. Animals That Jump
3. Hop! Hop! Hop!

Emily put on her blue coat and her fuzzy pink hat. Then she put on her warm, white mittens.

1. A Hot Day
2. Getting Ready to Go
3. Emily Likes to Play

Dan gave his pet dog a bone. He gave his fat cat some canned cat food. He also fed the ducks.

1. Feeding the Animals
2. Dan's Animals
3. Cats, Dogs, and Birds

Make these words plural, meaning more than one, by adding -s or -es.
Escribe el plural de estas palabras agregando –s o –es.

EXAMPLE:

1. cat _____cats_____
2. glass _____
3. truck _____
4. fan _____
5. wish _____
6. ball _____
7. box _____
8. bird _____

9. kitten _____
10. inch _____
11. dish _____
12. clock _____
13. bus _____
14. peach _____
15. brush _____
16. dog _____

Subtract and fill in the answers on the outer circle.
Resta y escribe las respuestas en el círculo exterior.

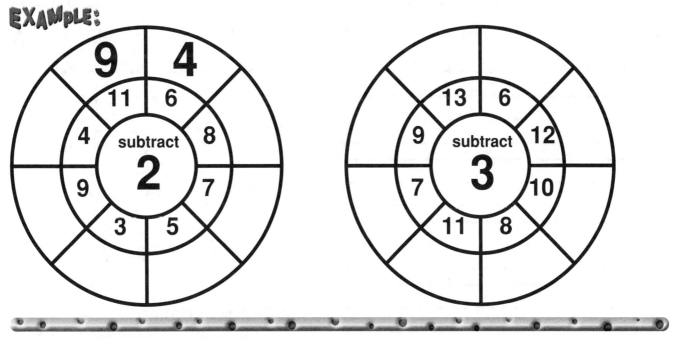

EXAMPLE:

Circle and write the word that goes with each picture.
Encierra en un círculo y escribe la palabra que coincide con cada dibujo.

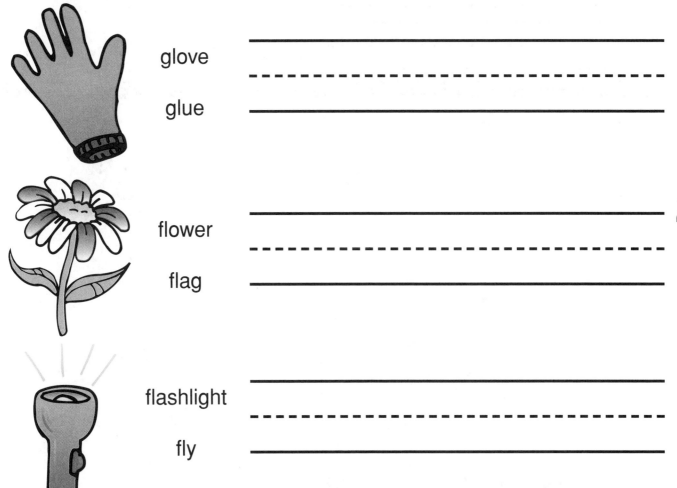

glove

glue

flower

flag

flashlight

fly

Date _____

Name _____

Use the following words to fill in the blanks:
Usa las siguientes palabras para completar los espacios en blanco:

Who	What	Where	Why	When

1. _____ are my keys?

2. _____ funny toy is mine?

3. _____ is your birthday party?

4. _____ is Mother coming?

5. _____ was there?

6. _____ is the sky dark?

Draw the other half. Color.
Dibuja la otra mitad. Colorea.

Solve the following problems.
Resuelve los siguientes problemas.

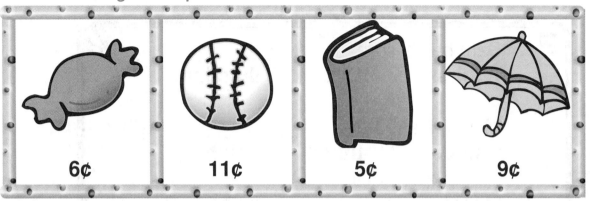

6¢   11¢   5¢   9¢

EXAMPLE:

Lisa has 15¢.
She bought an

$$\begin{array}{r} 15 \\ -\ 9 \\ \hline \end{array}$$

How much does she have left? **6¢**

Griffin bought a and a

How much did he spend?

Emily has 12¢.
She bought a

How much does she have left?

Trevor bought a and a

How much did he spend?

What month comes next? Fill in the blanks.
¿Qué mes viene después? Completa los espacios en blanco.

January	February	
April		June
		September
	November	

How many months are in a year? _____
¿Cuántos meses tiene un año? _____

Date _____

Name _____

© Federal Education Publishing   45   Level Blue

Write the correct word on each line.
Escribe la palabra correcta en cada línea.

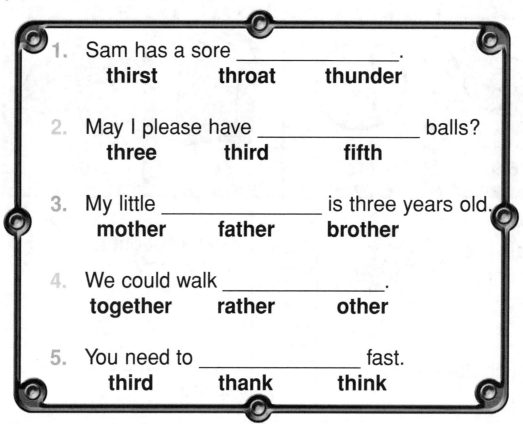

1. Sam has a sore _____.
   thirst   **throat**   **thunder**

2. May I please have _____ balls?
   three   **third**   **fifth**

3. My little _____ is three years old.
   mother   **father**   **brother**

4. We could walk _____.
   together   **rather**   **other**

5. You need to _____ fast.
   third   **thank**   **think**

Finish the story.
Termina la historia.

Last night I had the strangest dream. I dreamed that I...

Do a survey with your family and friends to see which flavor of popsicle is the most popular.

Realiza una encuesta para determinar qué sabor de helado es la más popular.

_____root beer   _____lime

_____orange   _____cherry

_____banana   _____grape

_____(others not listed)

Graph the results of your survey by placing an X on the coordinates of the number of people who liked each flavor.

Completa la gráfica con los resultados. Coloca una X en el número de personas a las que les gustaba cada sabor.

	1	2	3	4	5	6	7	8	9	10	11	12	13	14	15	16	17	18	19	20
Root Beer																				
Orange																				
Banana																				
Lime																				
Cherry																				
Grape																				
Other																				

What is your favorite flavor?   Which flavor was the least popular?

_____   _____

Which flavor was the most popular?

_____

Read, study, and spell.

Lee, estudia y deletrea.

1.	bake	bakes	baking	baked	baker
2.	walk	walks	walking	walked	walker
3.	stop	stops	stopping	stopped	stopper
4.	mix	mixes	mixing	mixed	mixer
5.	listen	listens	listening	listened	listener
6.	plant	plants	planting	planted	planter
7.	call	calls	calling	called	caller
8.	hug	hugs	hugging	hugged	hugger

Date

Name

Read the story; then answer the questions below.

Lee la historia y luego contesta las preguntas.

Mike lives on a farm. He wakes up early to do chores. Mike feeds the horses and pigs. He also collects the eggs. Sometimes, he helps his dad milk the cows. His favorite thing to do in the morning is eat breakfast.

1. Where does Mike live? _____

2. Why does he have to wake up early? _____

3. Name one chore Mike has to do: _____

4. What is his favorite thing to do in the morning?

    _____

Fill in the letters under the picture. Write the words on the correct line. Answer the puzzle below. Color each picture the color below its line.

Contesta la acertijo a continuación. Colorea cada dibujo del color indicado.

oi

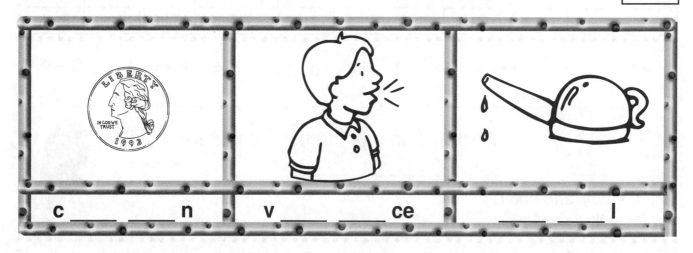

c ___ ___ n   v ___ ___ ce   ___ ___ l

_____ You can put this in your pocket.
    yellow

_____ You use this to hum, talk, and laugh.
    green

_____ Put this on and no more squeaks!
    red

Add.
Suma.

1.

2	1	4	5	2	4	5	3	8
2	1	4	5	3	3	4	5	0
+ 2	+ 1	+ 4	+ 5	+ 2	+ 0	+ 5	+ 3	+ 2

2.

3	6	7	10	8	5	9	2	4
3	6	0	10	3	1	0	3	4
+ 3	+ 6	+ 7	+ 10	+ 2	+ 5	+ 1	+ 7	+ 3

Give some facts about you and your family. Draw a picture of your family.
Proporciona algunos detalles sobre ti y tu familia. Haz un dibujo de tu familia.

1. I live in _____.
2. I have _____ sisters.
3. I have _____ brothers.
4. My mom's name is _____.
5. My dad's name is _____.

6. This summer we are going to _____.
7. I am _____ years old.
8. We have a pet _____.
9. My favorite food is _____.
10. My favorite color is _____.

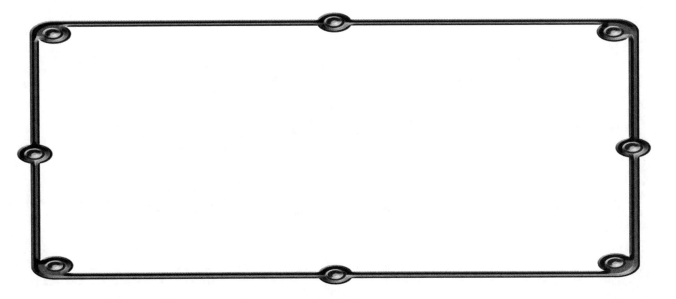

Date

Name

What day comes next? Fill in the blanks.

¿Qué día viene después? Completa los espacios en blanco.

Sunday, _____, _____,

Wednesday, _____, Friday, and

_____.

How many days are in a week? _____

Name the days you go to school during the week.

_____, _____,

_____, _____,

_____

Complete these sentences by unscrambling the words and writing them in the blanks.

Ordena las palabras y escríbelas en los espacios en blanco.

1. Mike had a _____ for _____ mother.
   igft   **ihs**

2. The _____ has a broken window.
   acr

3. A bee _____ on _____ flower.
   ats   **hte**

4. My _____ works at the _____.
   add   **tsoer**

5. Sue _____ a _____ dog named Spot.
   sha   **ept**

Add.
Suma.

5	8	3	9	15	10	8	9	6
+ 7	+ 4	+ 7	+ 5	+ 2	+ 6	+ 3	+ 4	+ 5

Subtract.
Resta.

12	9	11	8	10	6	7	12	10
- 8	- 4	- 7	- 8	- 2	- 2	- 5	- 4	- 6

Write the words that match the clues.
Escribe las palabras que coincidan con las pistas.

 EXAMPLE:

1. It begins like <u>stuck</u>. It rhymes with <u>late</u>.

   state

2. It begins like <u>rip</u>. It rhymes with <u>cake</u>.

   _____

3. It begins like <u>very</u>. It rhymes with <u>note</u>. _____

4. It begins like <u>break</u>. It rhymes with <u>him</u>. _____

5. It begins like <u>gum</u>. It rhymes with <u>late</u>. _____

6. It begins like <u>trip</u>. It rhymes with <u>rim</u>. _____

Date

Name

© Federal Education Publishing   Level Blue

Read the story below and then answer the questions.

Lee la historia y luego contesta las preguntas.

Ashley has a box of peaches. She wants to take the peaches home to her mother, so her mother can make a peach pie. Ashley says, "I love to eat peach pie!"

1. Who has a box of peaches?_____

2. Whom does she want to take the peaches to? _____

3. What does she want her mother to make? _____

4. Ashley says, "I love to eat _____!"

Complete the phrase below. Write at least three complete sentences.

Completa la frase a continuación. Escribe por lo menos tres oraciones completas.

I like myself because I can…

_____

_____

_____

_____

_____

_____

_____

Write the numeral by the number word.
Escribe el número que indica la palabra.

_____ six   _____ nine   _____ four   _____ seven

_____ ten   _____ two   _____ three   _____ one

_____ five   _____ eight   _____ zero   _____ twelve

_____ nineteen   _____ eleven   _____ fourteen

_____ twenty-one   _____ sixteen   _____ eighteen

_____ thirteen   _____ fifteen   _____ seventeen

_____ twenty   _____ twenty-five   _____ thirty

Does the y say ī or ē in the words below?
En estas palabras, la y ¿se pronuncia ī como
en <u>sky</u> o ē como en <u>any</u>?
Write ī or ē in the boxes.
Escribe ī o ē en los recuadros.

ī or ē

EXAMPLE:

ē					
bab<u>y</u>	fl<u>y</u>	wind<u>y</u>	bunn<u>y</u>	fr<u>y</u>	cherr<u>y</u>

sh<u>y</u>	famil<u>y</u>	sill<u>y</u>	happ<u>y</u>	jell<u>y</u>	pon<u>y</u>

cr<u>y</u>	m<u>y</u>	funn<u>y</u>	bu<u>y</u>	tr<u>y</u>	cand<u>y</u>

Date ____

Name ____

Draw the following.
Dibuja lo siguiente.

1. Draw one tree.
2. Draw four flowers.
3. Color one orange butterfly in the tree.

4. Draw a park bench.
5. Draw three pigeons beside the bench.
6. Draw a yellow sun.

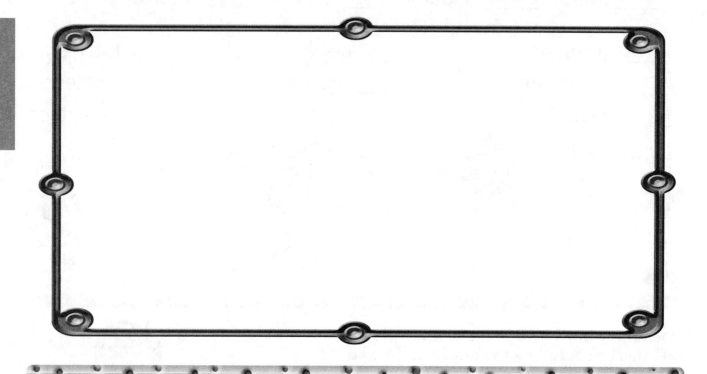

Read the story; then answer the questions.
Lee la historia y luego contesta las preguntas.

Sam is excited for summer. He wants to do many things. He wants to visit all of the animals at the zoo. He also wants to go camping in the mountains. Sam loves to swim and play with his friends, too.

1. What is Sam excited for? _____

2. What does he want to visit at the zoo? _____

3. Where does he want to go camping? _____

4. What does Sam love to do? _____

   and _____

Use the problems below to work on place value. Be sure to read before you write.

Usa los problemas de abajo para trabajar en el valor posicional. Lee antes de escribir.

46 = _____ tens _____ ones

19 = _____ ones _____ tens

84 = _____ tens _____ ones

64 = _____ tens _____ ones

7 tens and 6 ones =

4 tens and 0 ones =

1 ten and 1 one   =

9 ones and 3 tens =

1 hundred, 2 tens, and 8 ones = _____

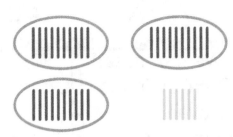

_____

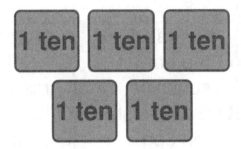

_____   _____

Circle the root, or base, word in each of the following words.

Círcula la raíz de cada una de las siguientes palabras.

EXAMPLE:

1. (run)ning	9. playful	17. friendly
2. hopped	10. boxes	18. rabbits
3. fastest	11. lovely	19. starry
4. standing	12. sickness	20. mopped
5. ripped	13. stepping	21. sadness
6. tallest	14. careful	22. missing
7. digging	15. dropped	23. bigger
8. slowly	16. catches	24. mixed

Date_____

Name_____

Fill in the circle in front of each correct answer. There may be more than one correct answer in each box.

Llena el círculo en frente de cada respuesta correcta.

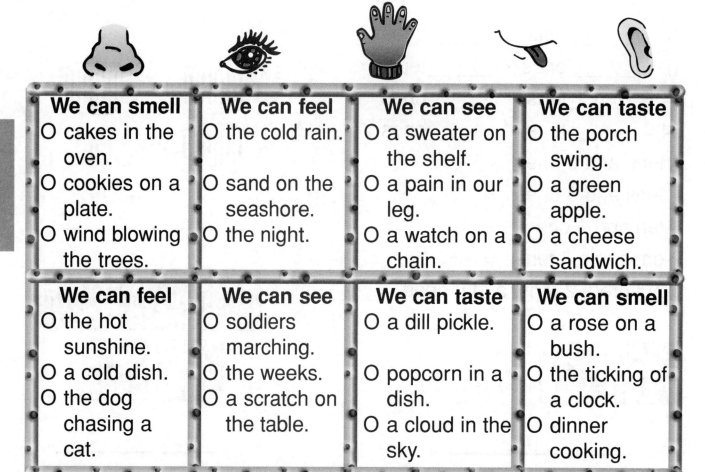

We can smell	**We can feel**	**We can see**	**We can taste**
O cakes in the oven.	O the cold rain.	O a sweater on the shelf.	O the porch swing.
O cookies on a plate.	O sand on the seashore.	O a pain in our leg.	O a green apple.
O wind blowing the trees.	O the night.	O a watch on a chain.	O a cheese sandwich.

We can feel	**We can see**	**We can taste**	**We can smell**
O the hot sunshine.	O soldiers marching.	O a dill pickle.	O a rose on a bush.
O a cold dish.	O the weeks.	O popcorn in a dish.	O the ticking of a clock.
O the dog chasing a cat.	O a scratch on the table.	O a cloud in the sky.	O dinner cooking.

If you planted a garden, what would you plant and why? Draw a picture.

¿Qué plantarías en un jardín? ¿Por qué? Haz un dibujo.

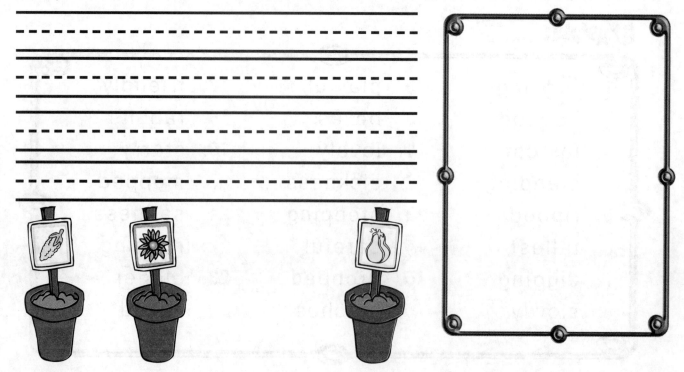

Solve these problems.
Resuelve estos problemas.

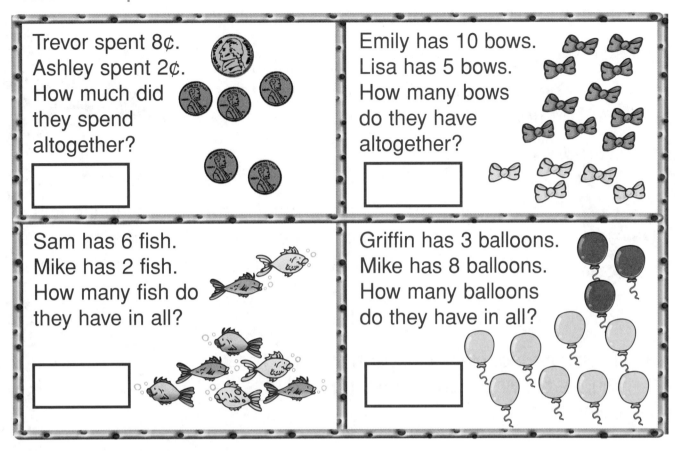

Trevor spent 8¢.
Ashley spent 2¢.
How much did
they spend
altogether?

Emily has 10 bows.
Lisa has 5 bows.
How many bows
do they have
altogether?

Sam has 6 fish.
Mike has 2 fish.
How many fish do
they have in all?

Griffin has 3 balloons.
Mike has 8 balloons.
How many balloons
do they have in all?

Study and spell the words in this word list.
Estudia y deletrea estas palabras.

brave	glad	stone	fast	crop	lost
slip	slap	last	step	stop	list

Unscramble the words. (Clue: You will find them in your word list.)
Ordena las palabras.

psla _____   etsno _____   stal _____

ptos _____   rebav _____   solt _____

porc _____   lgda _____   atsf _____

psil _____   epst _____   stil _____

Date

Name

Day 12

Read each paragraph and circle the sentence that explains the main idea of the paragraph.

Encierra en un círculo la oración que explique la idea principal del párrafo.

1. Emily's umbrella is old. It has holes in it. The color is faded. It doesn't keep the rain off her.

2. Tabby is a tan and white cat. He has a long, white tail. He lives on a farm in the country. Tabby helps the farmer by catching mice in the barn. He sleeps on soft, green hay.

3. There are big, black clouds in the sky. The wind is blowing, and it is getting cold. It is going to snow.

Find the opposites in the word search box.

Encuentra los opuestos en la sopa de letras.

1. The opposite of clean is _____.

2. The opposite of night is _____.

3. The opposite of hot is _____.

4. The opposite of light is _____.

5. The opposite of laugh is _____.

6. The opposite of up is _____.

v	d	i	r	t	y	e	h	k
a	b	a	m	c	e	u	d	g
x	c	r	y	o	d	s	a	j
w	l	h	o	l	r	j	y	n
q	a	z	c	d	d	o	w	n
d	a	r	k	b	s	s	l	m
h	r	e	p	s	t	d	j	p

Draw a line between the pairs that have the same answer.
Une con una línea los pares que tengan la misma respuesta.

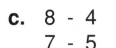

a. 5 - 3 ——— 6 - 4   **b.** 8 - 7   9 - 4
     3 - 3   9 - 1   3 - 1   5 - 3

c. 8 - 4   7 - 2   **d.** 8 - 2   8 - 3
     7 - 5   5 - 1   9 - 5   7 - 3

e. 10 - 5   7 - 1   **f.** 5 - 5   14 - 7
     12 - 6   9 - 4   12 - 9   8 - 5
     2 - 0   6 - 0   11 - 4   8 - 8

Something is wrong with one word in each sentence. Find the word and correct it!
En cada oración hay una palabra con un error. Encuéntralo y corrígelo.

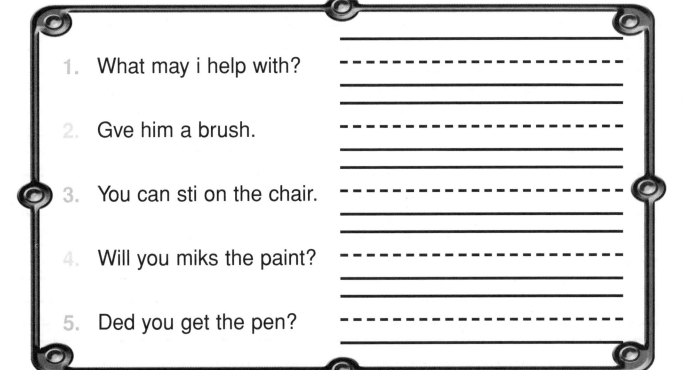

1. What may i help with?

2. Gve him a brush.

3. You can sti on the chair.

4. Will you miks the paint?

5. Ded you get the pen?

Date

Name

Day 13

Circle the words that do not belong in the numbered lists below.

Encierra en un círculo las palabras que no pertenezcan a la línea.

EXAMPLE:

1. beans   carrots   corn   (balls)   peas   (books)
2. train   boat   leg   car   dress   jet
3. cat   orange   green   blue   red   five
4. lake   ocean   pond   chair   river   shoe
5. bear   apple   lion   wolf   pillow   tiger
6. head   sleep   jump   hop   run   skip
7. Jane   Kathy   Tom   Fred   Jill   Anne
8. park   scared   happy   sad   mad   bee
9. tulip   daffodil   wagon   daisy   basket   rose
10. shirt   socks   bus   rope   pants   dress

Write a story that begins, "My favorite kind of fruit is _____ because..."

Escribe una historia que comience con: "My favorite kind of fruit is _____ because..."

Help the dogs find their doggy snacks by drawing a line to match each dog with the correct answer bone.

Une con una línea cada perro con el hueso con la respuesta correcta.

$$\begin{array}{r} 32 \\ -21 \\ \hline \end{array}$$

$$\begin{array}{r} 20 \\ -10 \\ \hline \end{array}$$

$$\begin{array}{r} 57 \\ -21 \\ \hline \end{array}$$

$$\begin{array}{r} 73 \\ -41 \\ \hline \end{array}$$

52   11   32   36   10   35

$$\begin{array}{r} 48 \\ -13 \\ \hline \end{array}$$

$$\begin{array}{r} 66 \\ -14 \\ \hline \end{array}$$

Circle the letters that spell the ending sounds.

Encierra en un círculo las letras que muestren los sonidos finales.

EXAMPLE:
math

$$\begin{array}{r} 12 \\ -2 \\ \hline 10 \end{array}$$

(th) sh ch   th sh ch   th sh ch   th sh ch   th sh ch

th sh ch   th sh ch   th sh ch   th sh ch   th sh ch

Date

Name

Fill in the missing oi or oy; then write the word.
Completa los <u>oi</u> u <u>oy</u> que falten y luego escribe la palabra.

b ___ ___

_____

s ___ ___ l

_____

___ ___ ster

_____

t ___ ___

_____

p ___ ___ nt

_____

Write the correct word in the blank.
Escribe la palabra correcta en el espacio en blanco.

1. Griffin _____ a song.   **sing   sang**

2. Did the bell _____ yet?   **ring   rang**

3. The bee _____ the king.   **stung   sting**

4. The waves will _____ the ship.   **sank   sink**

5. Mom will take a _____ trip.   **ship   short**

6. I _____ visit Grandma at home.   **shack   shall**

7. Lisa has a _____ on her back.   **rash   rush**

8. Trevor likes to _____ in the puddles.   **last   splash**

Finish the chart.
Termina los siguientes patrones.

1.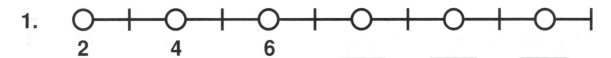

2.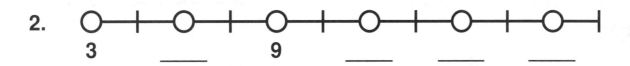

3.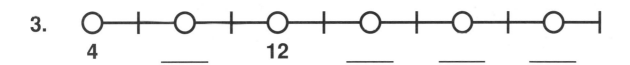

4.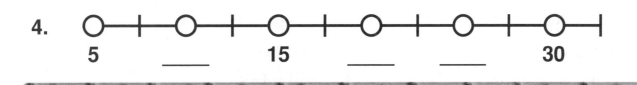

Use the Word Study List to do the following activity.
Usa la Lista de Estudio de Palabras para realizar esta actividad.

Word Study List

go
me
we
he
no
so
she
be
see
bee

1. Write the word <u>go</u>. Change the beginning letter to make two more words.

_____   _____   _____

2. Write the words that mean the opposite of <u>yes</u> and <u>stop</u>.

_____   _____

3. Write <u>she</u>, then write two more words that end the same.

_____   _____   _____

Date_____

Name_____

Fill in the blank with a homonym for the underlined word.
Remember: Homonyms sound the same but have different meanings.
Completa el espacio en blanco con un homónimo de la palabra subrayada.

made	new	~~eight~~	sea	through
wood	right	bee	hear	knot

EXAMPLE:

1. Ashley <u>ate</u> ___eight___ pancakes for breakfast.
2. Stay <u>here</u> and you can _____ the music.
3. Can you <u>see</u> the _____ from the top of the hill?
4. <u>Be</u> careful when you catch a _____ .
5. <u>Would</u> you get some _____ for the fire?
6. Did you <u>write</u> the _____ answer?
7. He <u>threw</u> the ball _____ the window.
8. Our <u>maid</u> _____ all the beds.
9. The little girl could <u>not</u> tie a _____ in the rope.
10. My mother <u>knew</u> the _____ teacher.

What did you do yesterday? Write down your activities in the order you did them.
Escribe lo que hiciste ayer en el orden en que lo hiciste.

1. _____
2. _____
3. _____
4. _____
5. _____
6. _____

Incentive Contract Calendar

Month (Mes) _____

My parents and I decided that if I complete 15 days of *Bridges*™ and read _____ minutes a day, my incentive/reward will be:

(Si yo completo 15 días de *Bridges*™ y leo _____ minutos al día, mi recompensa será:)

_____

Child's Signature (Firma del Niño)_____

Parent's Signature (Firma del Padre)_____

Day 1 (Día 1)	☆ 📖	_____
Day 2	☆ 📖	_____
Day 3	☆ 📖	_____
Day 4	☆ 📖	_____
Day 5	☆ 📖	_____
Day 6	☆ 📖	_____
Day 7	☆ 📖	_____
Day 8	☆ 📖	_____
Day 9	☆ 📖	_____
Day 10	☆ 📖	_____
Day 11	☆ 📖	_____
Day 12	☆ 📖	_____
Day 13	☆ 📖	_____
Day 14	☆ 📖	_____
Day 15	☆ 📖	_____

bridges

Parent: Initial the _____ for daily activities and reading your child completes.

Padre: (Marque _____ para las actividades y lectura que su niño complete.)

Child: Color the ☆ for daily activities completed.

Niño: (Colorea la ☆ para las actividades diarias que completes.)

Child: Color the 📖 for daily reading completed.

Niño: (Colorea el 📖 para las lecturas diarias que completes.)

Try Something New
Fun Activity Ideas

1 Play hopscotch, marbles, or jump rope.
Juega a la rayuela, a las canicas o a saltar la cuerda.

2 Visit a fire station.
Visita una estación de bomberos.

3 Make a map of you neighborhood.
Haz un mapa de tu vecindario.

4 Make up a song.
Inventa una canción.

5 Make a hut out of blankets and chairs.
Fabrica una choza con mantas y sillas.

6 Put a note in a helium balloon and let it go.
Coloca una nota en un globo de helio y déjalo ir.

7 Start a journal. Write about your favorite vacation memories.
Comienza un diario. Escribe sobre tus recuerdos favoritos del verano.

8 Make 3-D nature art. Glue leaves, twigs, dirt, grass, and rocks on paper.
Haz arte 3-D. Pega hojas, ramitas, tierra, césped y rocas en un papel.

9 Find an ant colony. Spill some food and see what happens.
Encuentra una colonia de hormigas. Derrama comida y observa qué sucede.

10 Play charades.
Juega a los acertijos.

11 Make up a story by drawing pictures.
Inventa una historia realizando dibujos.

12 Do something to help the environment. Clean up an area near your house.
Haz algo para ayudar al medioambiente. Limpia un área cercana a tu hogar.

13 Weed a row in the garden. Mom will love it!
Desmaleza una linea en el jardín. ¡A tu mamá le encantará!

14 Take a trip to a park.
Ve de paseo a un parque.

15 Learn about different road signs.
Aprende sobre las diferentes señales de tránsito.

Read and solve the math problem below.
Lee y resuelve este problema matemático.

On July 4th, Todd and his friends went to the parade. It was a hot day. Todd bought five snow cones. He gave one to Griffin, one to Ashley, and one to Emily. How many snow cones did Todd have left?

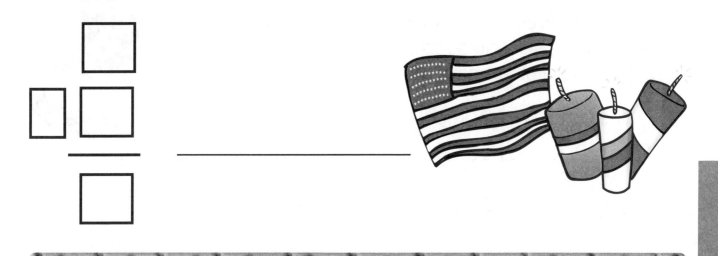

Divide the following compound words.
Divide estas palabras compuestas.

EXAMPLE: snow/ball

1. goldfish
2. blueberry
3. hairbrush
4. yourself
5. railroad
6. sometime

7. daytime
8. grapefruit
9. bedtime
10. popcorn
11. sailboat
12. today

13. spaceship
14. raindrop
15. newspaper
16. doghouse
17. cupcake
18. sidewalk

Date _____

Name _____

© Federal Education Publishing   Level Blue

Read and answer the questions.
Lee y contesta las preguntas.

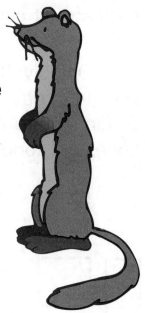

Years ago, many black-footed ferrets lived in the West. They were wild and free. Their habitat was in the flat grasslands. Their habitat was destroyed by man.

The ferrets began to vanish. Almost all of them died. Scientists worked to save the ferrets' lives, and now their numbers have increased.

1. Where did the black-footed ferrets live?

_____

2. Who worked to save the ferrets' lives?

_____

3. What happened when the scientists started to work?

_____

How many words can you make using the letters in "camping trip"?
¿Cuántas palabras puedes formar usando las letras en "camping trip"?

paint

_____

_____

_____

_____

Subtract.
Resta.

10	10	10	10	10	10	10	10	10
- 2	- 9	- 7	- 1	- 8	- 3	- 4	- 6	- 5

11	11	11	11	11	11	11	11	11
- 2	- 9	- 7	- 1	- 8	- 3	- 5	- 0	- 6

12	12	12	12	12	12	12	12	12
- 2	- 9	- 7	- 1	- 8	- 3	- 5	- 0	- 6

Write a story.
Escribe una historia.

If I were a firecracker, I would…

Date ___

Name ___

Number the sentences in their correct order.
Enumera las oraciones en el orden correcto.

_____ Lisa's friend made a wish and blew out the candles.

_____ Lisa put sixteen blue candles on the cake.

_____ Lisa made a chocolate cake for her friend.

_____ Lisa went to the store and bought a cake mix.

_____ Lisa lit the candles with a match.

Draw a picture of the birthday cake Lisa made for her friend.
Haz un dibujo de la torta de cumpleaños que preparó Lisa.

Match the sign shapes to the correct answer and then color the signs.
Une las señales con la respuesta correcta. Colorea las señales.

yield
yellow

hospital
blue

railroad crossing
black/white

phone
blue

stop
red

handicapped
blue

Which balloon has the number described by the tens and ones? Color that balloon. Use the color that is written in each box.

Colorea el globo que tiene el número que indican las decenas y unidades. Utiliza el color escrito en cada recuadro.

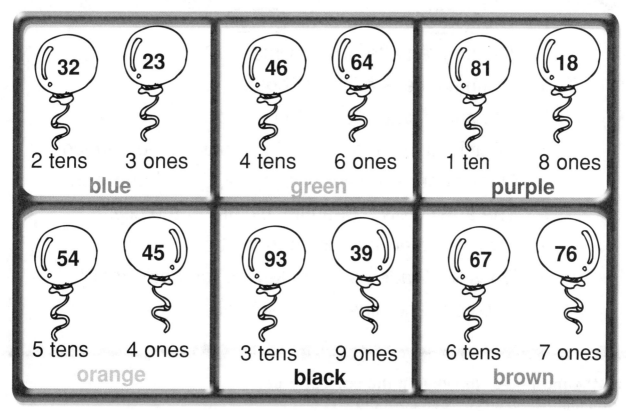

One word is misspelled in each sentence. Write the correct word from the list.

En cada oración hay una palabra está mal escrita. Escríbela correctamente. Usa la Lista de Palabras como ayuda.

Word Study and Spelling List

help

met

next

leg

pet

net

wet

1. A cat is a good pat.

2. She ran to get hlp.

3. He sat nekst to her.

4. We mit on the bus.

5. The dog cut his lag.

6. The duck got wit.

7. The fish is in the nut.

Date

Name

Read the sentences. Circle the nouns (naming words).

Lee las oraciones. Encierra en un círculo los sustantivos (palabras que nombran).

EXAMPLE:

1. The (horse) lost one of his (shoes)
2. The dog ran after the mailman.
3. A submarine is a kind of boat.
4. The nurse read a book to the sick lady.
5. What kind of sandwich did you have in your lunch?
6. Our teacher showed us a movie about butterflies.
7. The artist drew a beautiful picture of the city.
8. My little sister has a cute teddy bear.
9. Does Mr. Slade have the key for the back door?
10. The boys and girls left for school.

Write the months of the year in the correct order.

Escribe los meses en el orden correcto.

March	February	April	August
November	January	May	December
June	September	July	October

1. _____   7. _____
2. _____   8. _____
3. _____   9. _____
4. _____   10. _____
5. _____   11. _____
6. _____   12. _____

Name

Date

1. **Circle the odd numbers in each row.**
Encierra en un círculo los números impares de cada línea.

   a. 2   5   7   3   9   4   6   11

   b. 1   10   6   8   12   13   15   2

   c. 5   11   9   13   14   17   19   3

2. **Circle the even numbers in each row.**
Encierra en un círculo los números pares de cada línea.

   a. 6   9   2   11   4   7   3   8

   b. 13   8   10   6   12   16   9   5

   c. 14   16   9   11   12   18   7   4

3. **Circle the largest number in each set.**
Encierra en un círculo el número mayor de cada serie.

   a. 26 or 32   **c.** 51 or 49   **e.** 41 or 14

   b. 19 or 21   **d.** 80 or 60   **f.** 67 or 76

Write the middle consonant of each word below.
Escribe la consonante del medio de cada palabra a continuación.

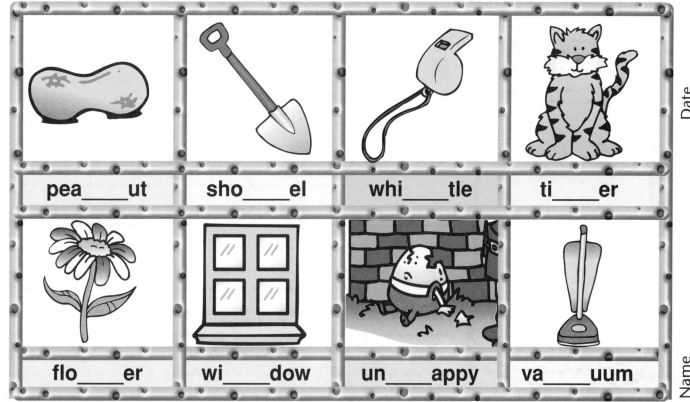

pea____ut   sho____el   whi____tle   ti____er

flo____er   wi____dow   un____appy   va____uum

Date_____

Name_____

Read each sentence. Write the correct word on the line.
Lee cada oración. Escribe la palabra correcta en la línea.

aw — hawk   au — auto   oi — oil   oy — boy

1. A dime is a _____.
   coin   point   lawn

2. I want to buy my friend a new _____.
   boy   toy   claw

3. My cat has one white _____.
   paw   saw   car

4. Don has two sons and one _____.
   paw   daughter   boil

Invent, design, and describe a new kind of soda pop!
¡Inventa, diseña y describe un nuevo tipo de gaseosa!

Fill in the blank space with a number to get the answer in the box.
Completa el espacio en blanco con un número para obtener la respuesta que aparece en el recuadro.

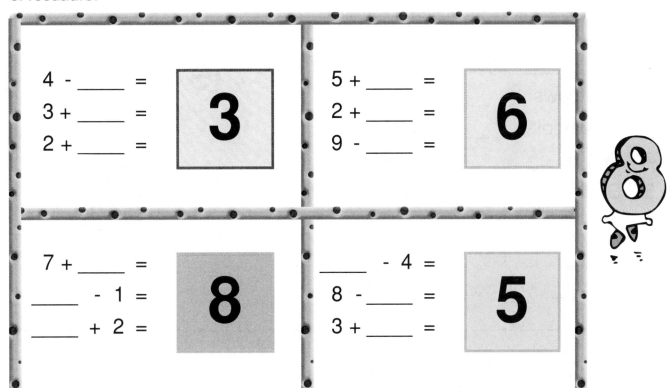

4 - ___ =
3 + ___ =
2 + ___ =

3

5 + ___ =
2 + ___ =
9 - ___ =

6

7 + ___ =
___ - 1 =
___ + 2 =

8

___ - 4 =
8 - ___ =
3 + ___ =

5

Fill in each blank with the correct contraction.
Escribe la contracción correcta.

Write the two words that make up the contraction.
Escribe las palabras que forman la contracción.

EXAMPLE:

1. can not _can't_

2. I am _____

3. you are _____

4. do not _____

5. he is _____

6. I will _____

7. you have _____

8. isn't _____

9. you've _____

10. she's _____

11. couldn't _____

12. we're _____

13. didn't _____

14. they'll _____

Date

Name

Fill in the blanks using is or are. On line 9, write a sentence using is. On line 10, write a sentence using are.

Completa los espacios en blanco con is o are. En la línea 9, escribe una oración utilizando is. En la línea 10, escribe una usando are.

1. We _____ going to town tomorrow.
2. The cows _____ in the field.
3. This book _____ not mine.
4. Where _____ a box of chalk?
5. Seals _____ fast swimmers.
6. _____ he going to help you?
7. It _____ very hot outside today.
8. _____ you going to the circus?
9. _____
10. _____

Read the sentences. Put a (.), (!), or (?) at the end of each one.

Lee las oraciones. Coloca un (.), (!) o (?) al final de cada una.

1. What time do you go to bed___
2. Why did the baby cry___
3. That girl over there is my sister___
4. We do not have our work done___
5. Get out of the way___
6. Are you and I going to the movie___
7. Go shut the door___
8. Do monsters have horns on their heads___
9. My parents are going on a long trip___
10. Look out___ That car will run you over___

Subtract.
Resta.

A.

15	14	16	17	13
- 4	- 2	- 8	- 3	- 4

B.

10	18	13	11	16
- 4	- 7	- 6	- 9	- 5

C.

17	12	10	18	19
- 8	- 5	- 1	- 4	- 9

Synonyms are words that have the same or nearly the same meaning. Find a synonym in the train for each of the words below. Write the word on the line.

Encuentra en el tren un <u>sinónimo</u> para cada palabra que aparece más abajo.
Escribe la palabra en el espacio en blanco.

happy   big
ill   start

easy   close
scared   large

tidy   copy
quick   funny

begin _____   afraid _____   trace _____

sick _____   shut _____   fast _____

glad _____   simple _____   silly _____

large _____   big _____   neat _____

© Federal Education Publishing   77   Level Blue

Date _____

Name _____

Unscramble the scrambled word in each sentence and write it correctly.

Ordena la palabra desordenada de cada oración y escríbela correctamente.

1. A <u>brzea</u> is an animal in the zoo.   _____

2. The robin has <u>nowlf</u> away.   _____

3. We mixed flour and eggs in a <u>owlb</u>.   _____

4. Button your button and zip your <u>rpzipe</u>.   _____

5. A lot of <u>leppeo</u> were at the game.   _____

6. We met our new teacher <u>yatdo</u>.   _____

7. My old <u>oessh</u> do not fit my feet.   _____

8. We made a list of <u>ngtihs</u> to get.   _____

9. Jim got <u>irtyd</u> when he fell in the mud.   _____

10. <u>eSktri</u> three and you're out.   _____

Draw a monster and label the following parts:

Dibuja un monstruo y ponle nombre a las siguientes partes:

stomach, forehead, tongue, throat, feet, arms, eyes, mouth, legs, nose, and any other parts you include.

Add.
Suma.

```
  3      6      9      5      4      2      3      5
  5      4      2      1      3      3      3      5
+ 2    + 3    + 2    + 2    + 4    + 5    + 4    + 3
```

```
  4      7      1      6      2      8      4      3
  5      2      8      1      3      2      2      7
+ 3    + 1    + 1    + 4    + 2    + 3    + 6    + 1
```

7 + 3 + 1 = _____   8 + 2 + 2 = _____   3 + 5 + 1 = _____

Read the sentences. Find a synonym for each underlined word. Write the new word on the lines. A synonym is a word that has the same or nearly the same meaning as another.

Encuentra un sinónimo para cada palabra subrayada. Escribe la nueva palabra en la línea.

automobile	small	glad	rush

The baby is very <u>tiny</u>.

_____

- - - - - - - - - - - - - - - - - - -

_____

The <u>car</u> ran out of gas.

_____

- - - - - - - - - - - - - - - - - - -

_____

Susan won, so she was very
<u>happy</u>.

_____

- - - - - - - - - - - - - - - - - - -

_____

My mother was in a big <u>hurry</u>.

_____

- - - - - - - - - - - - - - - - - - -

_____

Date

Name

Make an X by the answers to the questions.
Coloca una X delante de las respuestas a las preguntas.

How is a snake like a turtle?

_____ 1. They both have shells.

_____ 2. They both can be found on land.

_____ 3. They are both reptiles.

_____ 4. They both fly in the sky.

_____ 5. They both have tails.

_____ 6. They both eat flies.

_____ 7. They both have legs.

How is a bike like a truck?

_____ 1. They both have tires.

_____ 2. They both need gas.

_____ 3. They both can be differ- ent colors.

_____ 4. They can both be new and shiny.

_____ 5. They both have four wheels.

_____ 6. They both can go.

_____ 7. You can ride in both of them.

How is a sailor like a doctor?

_____ 1. They both wear white.

_____ 2. They both wear hats.

_____ 3. They both work with dogs.

_____ 4. They both are people.

_____ 5. Their job is to help sick peo- ple.

_____ 6. They have to work on a ship.

_____ 7. They both should be helpful.

Finish the story.
Termina la historia.

One day Ashley went out to play. Her friend, Lisa, was already outside.

Lisa said to Ashley, "Let's go play…"

_____

_____

_____

_____

_____

_____

_____

Color in the correct fraction of each picture.
Colorea la fracción correcta de cada dibujo.

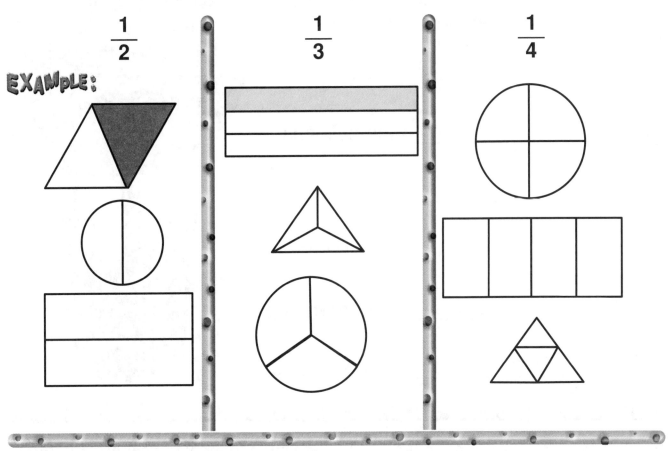

Color the matching bat and ball with the same color.
Colorea del mismo color los bates y pelotas que coincidan.

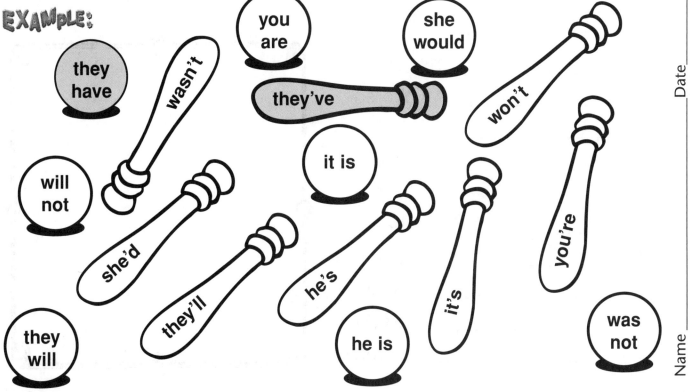

Date

Name

Day 8

Make up five funny sentences using one word from each column on the hot-air balloon. Do not use any of the words more than once.

Inventa cinco oraciones divertidas usando una palabra de cada columna del globo. Usa cada palabra solamente una vez.

children	held
robbers	fed
bugs	followed
bears	found
birds	dropped

1. _____ the balloons.

2. _____ a big truck.

3. _____ the silly cow.

4. _____ the green frog.

5. _____ all the people.

Read the words in the right column. Write the words in alphabetical order in the left column. Draw your favorite animal in the box.

Lee las palabras de la columna a la derecha. Escríbelas en orden alfabético en la columna a la izquierda.

1. _____ pig
2. _____ horse
3. _____ cat
4. _____ frog
5. _____ ant
6. _____ bear
7. _____ giraffe
8. _____ deer
9. _____ elephant
10. _____ monkey

Add or subtract.
Suma o resta.

11	18	3	10	17	13	18	19
+ 7	+ 1	+ 7	- 3	- 2	+ 6	- 6	- 7

33	64	5	2	12	14	27	16
+ 5	- 3	+ 3	+ 4	- 7	-11	- 3	- 8

17 + 2 = _____   11 - 3 = _____   13 + 5 = _____

Unscramble the words.
Ordena las palabras.

psto _____   ithkn _____

sfat _____   oonn _____

ltpae _____   ppayh _____

pste _____   seay _____

gbrni _____   dbyo _____

rdnki _____   stfri _____

enwt _____   yrc _____

© Federal Education Publishing   83   Level Blue

Date _____

Name _____

Read the words aloud; then write them in alphabetical order.

Lee las palabras en voz alta y luego escríbelas en orden alfabético.

rabbit

snake

lion

dog

fish

dish

make

candy

puppy

vase

1. _____

2. _____

3. _____

4. _____

5. _____

6. _____

7. _____

8. _____

9. _____

10. _____

Dairy Designs. A dairy company has asked you to create a design for a milk carton. Create and color an original milk carton design for the company.

Crea un diseño original de un envase de cartón para la leche.

Color the coins that match the given amount.
Colorea las monedas que correspondan a la cantidad dada.

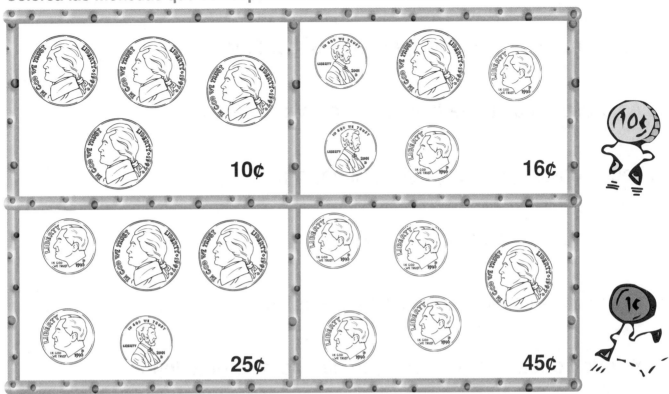

10¢

16¢

25¢

45¢

Match the homonyms. <u>Homonyms</u> are words that sound the same but have different meanings.
Une los homónimos.

EXAMPLE:

ate	heel		flower	through
cent	sea		threw	pair
knight	night		pain	hear
our	one		pear	flour
write	right		know	pane
knew	sent		here	male
heal	eight		maid	blew
see	hare		mail	no
hair	new		sail	made
won	hour		blue	sale

Date_____

Name

Read these silly sentences! Put a  **by your favorite sentence.**
¡Lee estas oraciones tontas! Coloca un al lado de tu oración favorita.

1. You can spend a day at the beach without money.

2. A yardstick has three feet, but it really cannot walk.

3. You might whip cream, but it will not cry.

4. It is not mean to beat scrambled eggs.

5. Rain falls sometimes, but it never gets hurt.

6. You do not eat a whole lot if you eat the hole of a donut.

Draw four things that belong in each box.
Dibuja cuatro cosas que correspondan a cada recuadro.

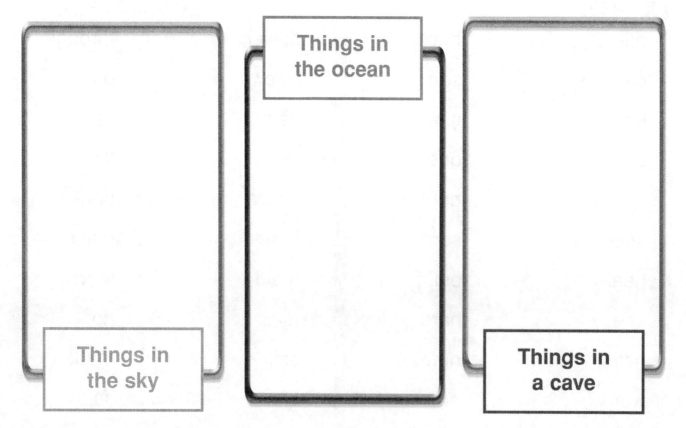

Things in
the ocean

Things in
the sky

Things in
a cave

Add or subtract.
Suma o resta.

1.
10	18	7	7	8	6	9	4	9
- 4	-14	- 3	+ 5	+ 2	- 4	- 4	+ 7	+ 2

2.
11	11	10	9	8	9	7	10	11
- 1	+ 8	- 8	+ 8	+ 2	+ 1	- 5	- 3	- 7

8 + 6 = _____   9 + 3 = _____   4 + 9 = _____

Antonyms. Match the words with opposite meanings.
Une las palabras con el significado opuesto.

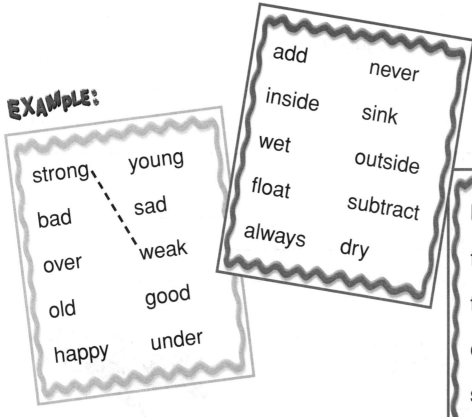

EXAMPLE:

strong   young
bad   sad
over   weak
old   good
happy   under

add   never
inside   sink
wet   outside
float   subtract
always   dry

light   thin
fat   off
tall   fast
on   dark
slow   short

Date _____

Name _____

Read each sentence. Do what it tells you to do. Then put a ✔ in the box to show that you have finished that step.

Haz lo que cada oración te diga que hagas. Coloca un ✔ en el recuadro luego de que lo hayas hecho.

Let's get ready for lunch.

☐ Draw a plate on the place mat.

☐ Draw a napkin on the left side of the plate.

☐ Draw a fork on the napkin.

☐ Draw a knife and spoon on the right side of the plate.

☐ Draw a glass of purple juice above the napkin.

☐ Draw your favorite lunch.

Enjoy!

Finish this story.
Finaliza la historia.

If I could fly anywhere, I would fly to _____

because... _____

_____

_____

_____

_____

_____

_____

_____

_____

_____

Finish each table.
Termina las tablas.

Add 10	
5	EX. 15
8	
7	
9	
3	
4	

Add 8	
2	
6	
4	
7	
3	
5	

Add 6	
10	
6	
8	
7	
4	
5	

Circle the correctly spelled word in each row.
Encierra en un círculo la palabra escrita correctamente en cada línea.

1. ca'nt	can'nt	can't	
2. esy	easy	eazy	
3. crie	cri	cry	
4. kea	key	kee	
5. buy	buye	biy	
6. lihg	light	ligte	
7. allready	already	alredy	
8. summ	som	some	
9. sekond	secund	second	
10. hasn't	has'nt	hasent	

11. wonce	onse	once	
12. pritty	preety	pretty	
13. carry	carey	carrie	
14. you're	yure	yo're	
15. parte	part	parrt	
16. star	stor	starr	
17. funy	funny	funnie	
18. babie	babey	baby	
19. mabe	maybe	maybee	
20. therde	therd	third	

Name

Date

© Federal Education Publishing   89   Level Blue

Circle the correct answer.
Encierra en un círculo la respuesta correcta.

1.	Another name for <u>boy</u> is:	girl	son	funny
2.	After seven comes:	six	nine	eight
3.	I bite with:	wheel	teeth	arms
4.	A car and truck roll on:	with	whip	wheels
5.	A farmer grows:	ship	wheat	land
6.	Your brain helps you:	this	thing	think
7.	A chair can also be a:	seat	sound	safe
8.	A rabbit has:	while	whirl	whiskers

Do the crossword puzzle.
Haz el crucigrama.

Word List

cent

sent

here

night

write

weight

Down

1. A penny is worth one _____.

2. My friend _____ me a letter.

3. Please _____ your name.

Across

1. Will you please come _____?

2. When the sun goes down, it is _____.

3. The doctor checked my _____.

Make number sentences. Use only the numbers in the circles.

Forma operaciones con los números. Usa solamente los números encerrados en los círculos.

EXAMPLE:

13
8   5

12
5   7

___8___ + ___5___ = ___13___

___ + ___ = ___

___ - ___ = ___

___ - ___ = ___

___ + ___ = ___

___ + ___ = ___

___ - ___ = ___

___ - ___ = ___

14
8   6

6   9
15

___ + ___ = ___

___ + ___ = ___

___ - ___ = ___

___ - ___ = ___

___ + ___ = ___

___ + ___ = ___

___ - ___ = ___

___ - ___ = ___

Put the words under the correct sound-picture.

Coloca las palabras bajo el dibujo del sonido correcto.

Word List

bone	fox
those	coat
log	rock
drove	top
job	rope
note	dock

long <u>o</u> (ō)  nose   short <u>o</u> (ŏ) pop

1.   1.

2.   2.

3.   3.

4.   4.

5.   5.

6.   6.

Date

Name

Circle and write the action verb in each sentence.
Encierra en un círculo y escribe el verbo activo de cada oración.

EXAMPLE:

1. The chicken (ran) away. _ran_____
2. Judy cut her finger with the knife._____
3. A kangaroo can hop very fast. _____
4. I like to swim in our pool. _____
5. Ted and Sid will chop some wood. _____
6. That kitten likes to climb trees._____
7. We will eat dinner at six o'clock. _____
8. The baby was yawning. _____
9. The car crashed into a tree. _____
10. Please peel this orange for me. _____

Draw a face beside each statement that tells how it makes you feel.
Al lado de cada oración, dibuja una cara que muestre como te hace sentir.

1. a rainy day

2. chocolate cake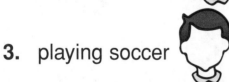

3. playing soccer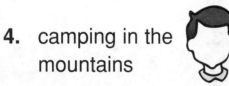

4. camping in the mountains

5. fighting with a friend

6. taking a bath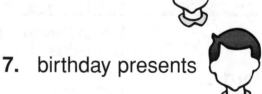

7. birthday presents

8. eating beans and corn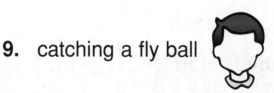

9. catching a fly ball

10. going to Grandmother's

Add.
Suma.

1. | 3 | 3 | 6 | 2 | 4 | 5 | 7 | 3 |
    | 2 | 4 | 1 | 2 | 3 | 4 | 1 | 5 |
    | + 1 | + 2 | + 2 | + 3 | + 3 | + 6 | + 2 | + 4 |

2. | 1 | 6 | 7 | 4 | 5 | 4 | 8 | 4 |
    | 3 | 3 | 2 | 5 | 2 | 4 | 1 | 6 |
    | + 2 | + 1 | + 1 | + 2 | + 3 | + 1 | + 2 | + 3 |

Write soft c words under pencil. Write hard c words under candy.
Escribe palabras con c suave bajo pencil. Escribe palabras con c fuerte bajo candy.

| grocery | cattle | cement | corn | price |
| cake | cellar | crib | grace | cow |

pencil    candy

1. _____   1. _____

2. _____   2. _____

3. _____   3. _____

4. _____   4. _____

5. _____   5. _____

Date _____

Name _____

Unscramble the sentences. Write the words in the correct order.
Ordena las oraciones. Escribe las palabras en el orden correcto.

1. sun shine will today The.

_____

2. mile today I a walked.

_____

3. house We painted our.

_____

4. Mother knit will I something for.

_____

Write a letter. Ask someone to a silly picnic.
Escribe una carta para invitar a alguien a un pic-nic absurdo.

Start your letter with "Dear _____,"
End your letter with "Yours truly, _____."

Color the shape that matches the description.
Colorea la figura que coincida con la descripción.

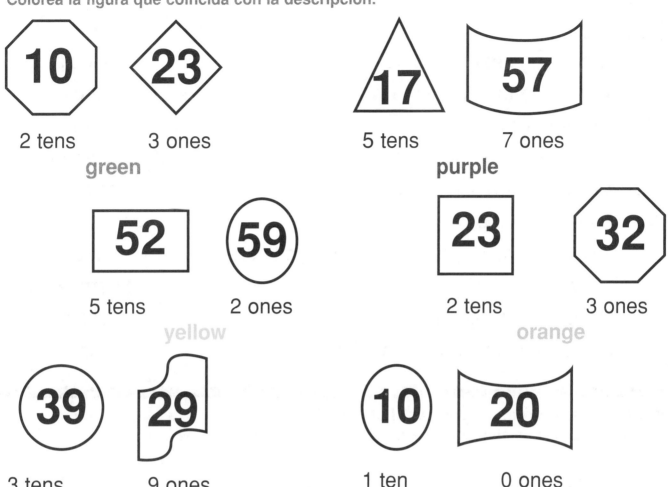

green — 2 tens (10), 3 ones (23)

purple — 5 tens (17), 7 ones (57)

yellow — 5 tens (52), 2 ones (59)

orange — 2 tens (23), 3 ones (32)

red — 3 tens (39), 9 ones (29)

blue — 1 ten (10), 0 ones (20)

Write each word under the correct sound-picture.
Escribe cada palabra bajo el dibujo del sonido correcto.

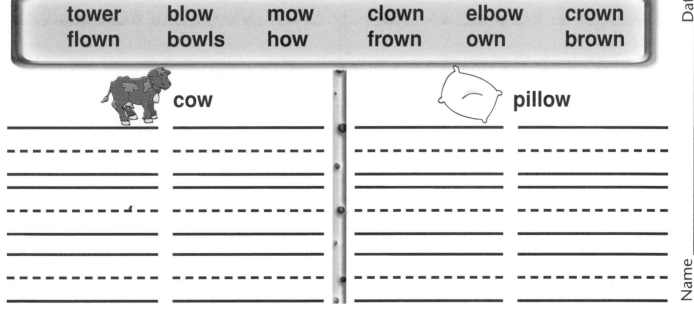

tower blow mow clown elbow crown
flown bowls how frown own brown

cow   pillow

Date

Name

Draw a line to the right word.
Dibuja una línea hasta la palabra correcta.

EXAMPLE:

1. Something near you is   clock
2. Something that tells time is a   bird
3. A time of day is   babies
4. A crow is a kind of   snoop
5. A place where fish live is an   close
6. Pork is a kind of   dusk
7. Chicks, ducklings, and fawns are kinds of   aquarium
8. A shop is a kind of   strike
9. To hit something is to   store
10. To look in someone else's things is to   meat

Write as many words as you can that describe…
Escribe todas las palabras que puedas para describir estas cosas.

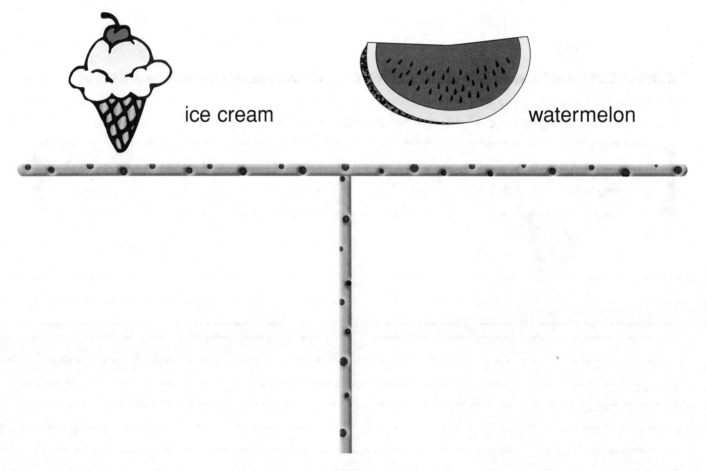

ice cream   watermelon

High-Frequency Word List

a	four	me	that
about	friends	my	the
after	from	new	their
again	funny	no	them
all	get	not	then
am	give	now	there
an	go	of	they
and	going	old	think
any	good	on	this
are	got	once	three
as	had	one	time
ask	has	open	to
at	have	or	too
ate	he	other	two
away	help	our	up
back	her	out	very
be	here	over	walk
because	him	people	want
big	his	play	was
black	home	please	we
blue	house	pretty	well
brown	how	put	went
but	I	ran	were
by	if	red	what
came	in	ride	when
can	into	round	where
charge	is	run	white
come	it	said	who
could	jump	say	will
day	know	school	win
did	last	see	with
do	let	she	would
down	like	so	yellow
eat	little	some	yes
every	live	soon	you
find	look	stop	your
fly	make	take	
for	may	thank	

Words to Sound Out, Read, and Spell

short ă words

can	mad
cap	gas
fan	sad
lap	ax
man	bag
map	tax
ran	rag
nap	wax
bad	tag
tap	cab
dad	wag
yap	jab
had	gag
has	nab

short ĕ words

bet	fed
beg	vet
get	led
leg	set
jet	wed
peg	wet
let	hen
hem	yet
met	pen
pep	ten
net	
web	
bed	
yes	

short ĭ words

bit	him
bib	hip
fit	rim
rib	lip
mitt	bid
fib	sip
hit	hid
mix	rip
pit	kid
six	tip
quit	lid
fix	zip
sit	did
dim	quip
dip	rid

short ŏ words

dog	pop
ox	hot
fog	rod
box	lot
log	pod
fox	tot
jog	cot
mob	dot
hop	not
rob	got
mop	pot
sob	
top	
job	

short ŭ words

bug	sum
rut	rug
dug	gum
bun	tug
hug	bus
fun	lug
jug	tub
run	but
mud	sub
sun	cut
dud	rub
cup	nut
hum	cub
pup	
mum	
mug	

-ll words

bill	tell
fill	well
dill	yell
hill	bell
spill	fell
will	dull
quill	doll
sell	

-ss words

pass	kiss
mass	miss
boss	bliss
moss	fuss
toss	muss
loss	less
hiss	mess

-ck words

back	peck
pack	duck
dock	deck
quack	luck
lock	kick
rack	tuck
sock	lick
tack	pick
rock	sick
neck	quick
buck	wick

-ff words

buff	huff
cuff	puff

L- Blends to Read!

fl-	sl-	cl-	pl-	bl-	gl-
flat	slab	class	plan	black	glum
flag	slack	clap	plat	bled	glut
flap	slam	clam	pled	bless	gloss
fled	slap	click	plot	bliss	glass
flex	sled	cliff	plop	blob	glad
flick	slick	clip	pluck	block	glory
flip	slid	clock	plum	blot	glow
flock	slim	clog	plug	bluff	
floss	slip	club	plus		
flop	slot	cluck			
fluff	slug				
flux					

R- Blends to Read!

gr-		br-	fr-	dr-	tr-	cr-	pr-
grab	grill	brag	free	drag	track	crab	practice
grape	grip	brake	fret	drab	trap	crack	prince
grass	grog	brand	frill	dress	trick	crib	price
grid	grub	brass	frog	drill	trip	crick	pray
grim	gruff	brave	from	drip	trim	cross	praise
grin		brick	fry	drop	trot	crop	prairie
				drug	truck		present
				drum			

Words to Sound Out, Read, and Spell

ar
car	harm	chart
far	charm	party
jar	barn	bark
star	yarn	dark
scar	art	mark
yard	dart	park
card	cart	shark
hard	part	spark
arm	smart	
farm	start	

or
for	born	dorm
fort	corn	form
sort	worn	torch
short	thorn	porch
sport	north	order
cork	forth	organ
fork	forty	story
pork	horse	history
stork	storm	

er
her
clerk
perch
nerve
verb
fern
were
serve

ir
dirt
shirt
first
third
swirl
skirt
firm
bird
thirst
twirl

ur
hurt
spurt
burnt
burp
curl
turtle
purple
church

Remember these special sounds!

sh
shed	brush
shell	slash
ship	flash
shack	clash
shag	trash
shin	crash
shock	smash
shot	fish
shop	dish
shuck	fresh
wish	
hush	
mush	
rush	

ch
check	inch
chess	pinch
chick	chug
chill	chap
chin	chaff
chip	
chop	
chum	
chat	
much	
such	
rich	
which	

th
this
them
that
thud
math
with
moth
thin
then
thick
bath
path
cloth
path

tch
hatch
patch
stitch
scotch
catch
ditch

wh
when
where
whip
why
what

Compound words surprise us!
pancake	rosebud
cupcake	bluebird
handshake	blueberry
cannot	frostbite
sunset	potpie
suntan	necktie
sandbox	wishbone
swingset	fireman
pineapple	nickname
sunrise	drumstick
sunshine	checkup
underline	
tiptoe	
bathrobe	

Here are -nt, -nd, -nk, and -ng words.

-nt
ant	spent
pant	mint
plant	hint
bent	print
dent	flint
rent	hunt
sent	stunt
tent	punt
vent	runt
went	

-nd
and	blond
band	end
hand	bend
sand	send
land	lend
stand	tend
grand	spend
bond	wind
pond	fund

-nk
bank	wink
yank	blink
sank	drink
tank	stink
drank	think
crank	honk
spank	bunk
ink	junk
pink	drunk
sink	skunk

-ng
bang	long
rang	strong
hang	king
hung	sing
sung	wing
stung	bring
flung	swing
swung	thing
gong	

What about -y at the end of words?
any	penny
many	puppy
very	sloppy
messy	happy
sticky	cherry
windy	angry
sandy	hungry
handy	sixty
copy	fifty
body	day
daddy	say
muddy	clay
candy	sway
twenty	may
dizzy	way
yummy	stay
funny	away
sunny	

These, too, are interesting!
key	donkey	monkey	turkey
keys	donkeys	monkeys	turkeys

Words to Sound Out, Read, and Spell

Magic e

can	cane
mad	made
cap	cape
man	mane
tap	tape
past	paste
bit	bite
kit	kite
quit	quite
win	wine
rip	ripe
hid	hide
grip	gripe
slid	slide

Long ā words to know!

bake	brake	cave	rake
pale	shape	wake	blaze
state	chase	tape	rate
shade	brave	waste	plane
name	plate	wave	taste
make	made	flake	gave
scale	game	drape	snake
late	lake	vase	scrape
mane	whale	came	base
frame	date	cake	shave
shake	cane	sale	awake
cape	blame	skate	grape
paste	take	trade	
save	glaze	same	

Long Ī words

dive	pride	pipe	hide
bite	wipe	while	chime
time	spike	slide	tribe
tire	pie	like	shine
line	tie	die	smile
live	dime	glide	wide
quite	hire	gripe	trike
crime	hive	size	alike
wife	white	prize	stripe
pine	slime	mine	strike
pile	life	five	lie
side	nine	kite	inside
hike	mile	lime	swipe
alive	ride	wire	
ripe	bike	fine	
file	bribe	drive	

Long ō words

rope	wore	hose	home
more	rose	those	
slope	chore	toe	
store	stole	code	
pose	smoke	tone	
quote	bone	drove	
doze	wove	throne	
rode	zone	pole	
stone	stove	mole	
dove	cone	joke	
shone	poke	shore	
hole	froze	note	
chose	hope	those	
hoe	sore	sole	
tore	nose	swore	
scope	score	woke	

ŌK, I know I can do it!

bow	slow	mellow
low	elbow	blow
mow	fellow	
grow	yellow	
snow	willow	
show	pillow	
throw	hallow	
bowl	flow	
own	tomorrow	
grown	rainbow	
thrown	snowman	
flown	window	
blown	widow	

These words say ō, too!

no
so
go
hello
Jell-O
Eskimo
hippo
lingo
jumbo
lasso
banjo
condo

ow and ou

ow

cow	crowd	growl
down	power	prowl
town	shower	chow
gown	towel	brow
clown	now	allow
crown	how	powder
drown	plow	drowsy
frown	owl	chowder
brown	howl	

ouch

out	found	mouse
shout	round	sour
about	sound	flour
trout	pound	ground
scout	count	account
loud	mount	thousand
cloud	around	discount
aloud	surround	county
bound	house	

oi words

oil	join
boil	joint
coil	point
soil	appoint
broil	disappoint
spoil	poison
void	
coin	

Glossary

a breve (ă) — el sonido <u>a</u> en <u>bat</u>.

a larga (ā) — el sonido <u>a</u> en <u>cake</u>.

abreviatura (abbreviation) — forma corta de una palabra. Por ejemplo: dic. por diciembre, Dr. por doctor. Las abreviaturas finalizan con un punto y muchas veces comienzan con mayúscula.

adjetivo (adjective) — una palabra que califica a un sustantivo o pronombre. Los adjetivos pueden describir cuántos, de qué tipo o cuál. En la oración "El hombre delgado cepillaba tres perros con un peine azul", tres, delgado y azul son adjetivos.

adverbio (adverb) — una palabra que modifica o califica a un verbo, adjetivo u otro adverbio. Los adverbios pueden indicar cómo, cuándo y dónde. En inglés, muchos finalizan en –ly, en español, muchos finalizan en –mente.

analogía (analogy) — una comparación entre dos pares de palabras. Por ejemplo, "la manzana es al árbol como la leche a la vaca" es una analogía que compara de dónde provienen dos cosas.

antónimo (antonym) — una palabra que significa lo opuesto a otra palabra. Contento y triste son antónimos.

área (area) — la medida de la superficie de un objeto. Calculamos el área multiplicando el largo por el ancho del objeto. El área se mide en unidades cuadradas. Entonces si el área de la superficie de una mesa mide 4 pies de largo y 3 pies de ancho, tendrá 12 pies cuadrados (3 x 4 = 12).

cambio físico (physical change) — ocurre cuando una sustancia cambia pero no se forma una nueva. Por ejemplo, un cambio físico ocurre cuando el agua se convierte en hielo.

cambio químico (chemical change) — ocurre cuando dos o más sustancias se combinan y forman una nueva sustancia. Por ejemplo, hierro más oxígeno forma óxido.

categorizar (categorize/categorizing) — agrupar ítems basándose en aspectos que tienen en común. Por ejemplo, se puede incluir manzanas, peras y bananas en una categoría que se denomine "Frutas".

circunferencia (circumference) — la distancia alrededor de un círculo. Para encontrar la circunferencia de un círculo se debe multiplicar el diámetro por 3.14.

cociente (quotient) — el resultado de un problema de división.

comillas (" ") (quotation marks) — las comillas se sitúan antes y después de lo que una persona está diciendo y, además, en los títulos de historias, poemas y canciones.

contracción (contraction) — una combinación reducida de dos palabras que incluye un apóstrofe en el lugar dónde se han omitido letras. "Didn't" es una contracción de "did not".

cursiva (cursive) — una forma de escritura en la que las letras están unidas: *esto es letra cursiva*.

diferencia (difference) — la respuesta a un problema de sustracción.

doble negación (double negative) — el uso de dos palabras negativas, como "not" o "no", cuando se necesita solamente una. Por ejemplo: "He did not have no breakfast," debería escribirse "He had no breakfast" o "He did not have any breakfast."

e breve (ĕ) — el sonido <u>e</u> en <u>pet</u>.

e larga (ē) — el sonido <u>e</u> en <u>sleep</u>.

estimar (estimate) — realizar una buena aproximación.

examen de desarrollo (essay test) — un examen en el que deben contestarse las preguntas en oraciones y párrafos.

examen objetivo (objective test) — un examen en dónde se debe responder verdadero o falso, multiple choice, unir, etc., en vez de desarrollar una respuesta.

Glossary

forma estándar / notación estándar (standard form / standard notation) — la forma habitual de escribir un número. 538 ó 6,700 están escritos en notación estándar.

fracción (fraction) — un número que representa parte de un total. 1/2 2/10 y 2/3 son fracciones.

frase preposicional (prepositional phrase) — una preposición y su objeto. En la oración "El gusano está en la manzana", "en la manzana" es la frase preposicional.

grupos consonánticos (blends) — dos consonantes que se juntan para formar un cierto sonido. Pl, br, gr, cl y sp son todos grupos consonánticos.

homófonos (homophones) — ver homónimos.

homónimos (también homófonos) (homonyms or homophones) — palabras que suenan o se escriben igual pero tienen un significado distinto. Por ejemplo: see y sea en inglés, echo y hecho en español.

i breve (ĭ) — el sonido i en pit.

i larga (ī) — el sonido i en ice.

idea principal (main idea) — la idea principal indica de qué trata una historia.

lluvia de ideas (brainstorm) — lanzar ideas.

modismo (idiom) — un dicho de una lengua que significa algo diferente a lo que las palabras realmente dicen. Por ejemplo, "llueven sapos y culebras" significa que está lloviendo muy fuerte, no que están cayendo animales del cielo.

múltiplo (multiple) — un número exactamente divisible por otro número. Por ejemplo: 6, 12 , 18 , 24 ,30 son todos múltiplos de 6.

número negativo (negative number) — un número menor a 0.

número positivo (positive number) — un número mayor a cero.

o breve (ŏ) — el sonido o en pot.

o larga (ō) — el sonido o en boat.

objeto directo (direct objects) — sustantivos o pronombres que completan o reciben la acción del verbo. En la oración "Él tiró la pelota," pelota es el objeto directo.

oración (sentence) — un grupo de palabras que expresa un pensamiento completo. Una oración comienza con mayúscula y, generalmente, finaliza con un punto (.), signo de interrogación (?), o signo de exclamación (!)

oración principal (topic sentence) — una oración que indica la idea principal de un párrafo.

palabra base (o palabra raíz) (base word or root word) — una palabra a la que puede agregársele un prefijo o un sufijo. Por ejemplo, "thank" sería la palabra base en "unthankful" y "gracia" sería la palabra base en "desgraciado".

palabra compuesta (compound word) — una palabra formada por dos palabras más pequeñas como, por ejemplo, "farmhouse" o "lightbulb" en inglés, "portalámpara" o "cubrecama" en español.

palabra raíz (o palabra base) (root word or base word) — una palabra a la que puede agregársele un prefijo o un sufijo. Por ejemplo "thank" sería la palabra base en "unthankful" y "gracia" sería la palabra base en "desgraciado".

perímetro (perimeter) — la distancia alrededor de un objeto, o el largo de todos sus lados. Para obtener el perímetro, se debe sumar el largo de todos los lados.

plural (plural) — más de uno.

polígono (polygon) — una figura cerrada por cuatro líneas rectas.

porcentaje (percent) — una porción de 100. Por ejemplo, 15% significa lo mismo que 15/100 ó 15 de 100.

predicado (predicate) — indica al lector algo sobre el sujeto de una oración.

Glossary

prefijo (prefix) —una sílaba que se agrega al principio de una palabra base para formar una nueva palabra. En la palabra "untie", -un es un prefijo, en la palabra "insatisfecho", -in es un prefijo.

preposición (preposition) — palabras como en, bajo y sobre, que muestran relaciones entre otras palabras. Por ejemplo "El gusano está en la manzana."

producto (product) — el resultado de un problema de multiplicación.

pronombre (pronoun) — una palabra que reemplaza a un sustantivo. Yo, él, ellos, alguien y nosotros son todos pronombres.

pronombre posesivo (possessive pronoun) — un pronombre que muestra posesión. Suyo, nuestro y suyos son pronombres posesivos.

pronombre subjetivo (subject pronoun) — pronombres como yo, tu, él, nosotros y ellos pueden ser el sujeto de una oración.

reagrupar (regroup) — en matemática, se reagrupa cuando se "toma prestado" diez de una columna para usarlo en otra. Por ejemplo, en el problema 22-17 se mueve 1 grupo de 10 de la columna de las decenas a la columna de las unidades, para poder restar 7 a 12. Entonces queda 1 decena en la columna de las decenas y 1 menos 1 es cero.

redondear (round(ing) numbers) — una manera de estimar números para que sea más fácil utilizarlos para resolver un problema. Por ejemplo, podría redondearse el número 9 "para arriba" a 10 o el número 103 "para abajo" a 100 ó 6.72 a 7 para ayudar a realizar rápidamente un estimativo.

schwa — el sonido "uh"

sílaba (syllable) — una combinación de letras que se pronuncian como una unidad y se utilizan para dividir palabras. "Perro" tiene dos sílabas (pe-rro), "camello" tiene tres sílabas (ca-me-llo) y "elefante" tiene cuatro (e-le-fan-te).

sílaba tónica (stressed syllable) — una sílaba que se enfatiza más que las otras cuando se pronuncia una palabra. Por ejemplo, cuando se dice fútbol, se pone un poco más de énfasis en la sílaba "fút" que en "bol". Pruébalo de una manera diferente y escucha como suena.

simplificación (fracciones) (reduce (fractions)) — escribir una fracción en su forma más simple, en la que el divisor común máximo del nominador y el denominador sea 1. Por ejemplo, en la fracción 6/9, tanto 6 como 9 pueden dividirse por 3, lo que da como resultado 2/3. 2 y 3 sólo pueden dividirse por el número 1, por lo tanto 2/3 es la forma más simple de escribir 6/9.

singular — uno.

sinónimo (synonym) — una palabra que significa prácticamente lo mismo que otra. Feliz y contento son sinónimos.

sufijos (suffixes) — una sílaba que se agrega al final de una palabra base para formar una nueva palabra. En la palabra "helpless", "less" es un sufijo, en la palabra "cordialmente", "-mente" es un sufijo.

sujeto (subject) — indica sobre qué o quién es la oración.

suma (sum) — el resultado de un problema de adición.

sustantivo (noun) — una palabra que nombra a una persona, lugar, cosa o idea. Mamá, castillo, tenedor y justicia son sustantivos.

sustantivo común (common noun) — un sustantivo que no es el nombre específico de una persona, lugar o cosa. Bebé, tienda, equipo e independencia son todos sustantivos comunes. Los sustantivos comunes no se escriben con mayúscula, salvo que sean la primera palabra de una oración.

sustantivo posesivo (possessive noun) — un sustantivo que muestra posesión. Por ejemplo, en la frase "the dog's dish", "dog's" es un posesivo porque indica que el plato (dish) pertenece al perro (dog). Para formar un

Glossary

sustantivo singular posesivo se agrega 's — dog's dish. Un sustantivo plural posesivo se forma agregando s' — dogs' dish (lo que significa que el plato es usado por más de un perro).

sustantivo propio (proper noun) — el nombre específico de una persona, lugar o cosa. Por ejemplo, Rob, New York, y Oreo son todos sustantivos propios. Los sustantivos propios siempre comienzan con mayúscula.

término de la preposición (object of a preposition) — el sustantivo o pronombre que sigue a una preposición. En la oración "El gusano está en la manzana", manzana es el término de la preposición en.

transformar a número mixto (fracciones) (renaming fractions) — convertir una fracción con un numerador mayor que su denominador en un número entero y una fracción. Por ejemplo, 10/6 puede transformarse a número mixto como 1 4/6 ó 1 2/3.

transportar (suma / multiplicación) (carry [addition/multiplication]) — como reagrupar, cuando uno transporta, mueve un número de una columna a otra. Por ejemplo, en 15 + 16, se suma 5 +6, lo que da por resultado 11. Piensa en 11 como 10 + 1. Para finalizar el problema se pone el 1 en el lugar de las unidades y luego se "transporta" el 10 a la columna de las decenas, donde ahora figuran 3 decenas, o 30. Por lo tanto, el resultado es 31.

u breve (ŭ) — el sonido "u" en cup.

u larga (ū) — el sonido "u" en blue.

valor relativo (place value) — se refiere al valor de un número basado en su posición dentro de un número mayor. Por ejemplo, en el número 245, el 5 se encuentra en el lugar de las unidades y representa 5 unidades, el 4 ocupa el lugar de las decenas y representa 40 ó 4 decenas y el 2 está ubicado en el lugar de las centenas, representando 200 ó 2 centenas.

verbo (verb) — palabras que muestran una acción o un estado. Saltar, pensar, ir, es y poder son todos verbos.

verbo 'to be' ('to be" verb) — una forma del verbo que significa ser, estar o existir: is, am, are, was, were, be, being, been.

verbo activo (action verb) — una palabra para algo que se realiza. Por ejemplo: correr, gritar o dormir son verbos activos.

verbo irregular (irregular verb) — los verbos regulares muestran que la acción sucedió en el pasado agregando –ed a la palabra base. Para mostrar el tiempo pasado en los verbos irregulares, se debe cambiar la ortografía. Por ejemplo, el tiempo pasado de "run" es "ran", no "runned" y el tiempo pasado de "go" es "went".

verbos auxiliares (helping verb) — verbos que "ayudan" al verbo principal. El verbo principal muestra la acción. En la oración "El puede ir mañana", ir es el verbo principal y puede es el verbo auxiliar.

verbos copulativos (state-of-being verbs) — indican lo que algo o alguien es o hace. Son verbos copulativos: ser, parecer y semejar.

verbos en tiempo pasado (past tense verbs) — palabras que describen acciones que ya sucedieron. Escribió, caminó, olió y miró, son todos verbos en tiempo pasado.

verbos en tiempo presente (present tense verbs) —verbos que ocurren ahora. Escribe, camina y mira son todos verbos en tiempo presente.

vocal sorda (silent vowel) — una vocal como "e" al final de "cake" que no tiene sonido cuando se pronuncia la palabra.

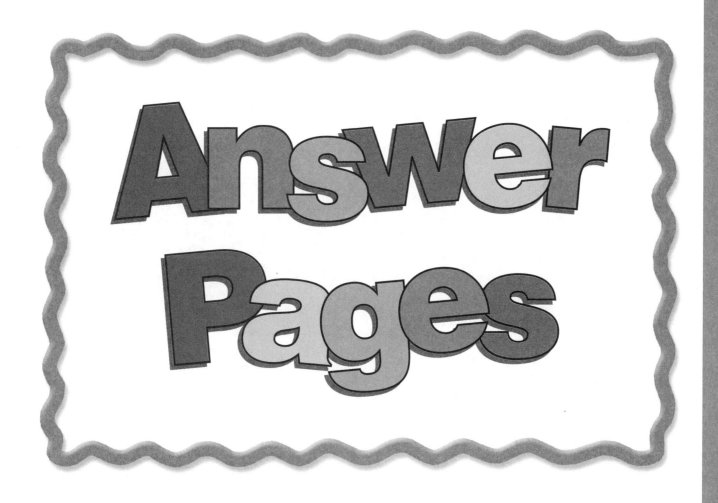

Write to 100.
Escribe hasta 100.

1	2	3	4	5	6	7	8	9	10
11	12	13	14	15	16	17	18	19	20
21	22	23	24	25	26	27	28	29	30
31	32	33	34	35	36	37	38	39	40
41	42	43	44	45	46	47	48	49	50
51	52	53	54	55	56	57	58	59	60
61	62	63	64	65	66	67	68	69	70
71	72	73	74	75	76	77	78	79	80
81	82	83	84	85	86	87	88	89	90
91	92	93	94	95	96	97	98	99	100

Circle the first letter underneath each picture if the picture begins with that sound. Circle the second letter if it ends with that sound. Color the pictures.
Encierra en un círculo la primera letra debajo del dibujo si éste comienza con ese sonido en inglés. Encierra en un círculo la segunda letra si el dibujo termina con ese sonido. Colorea los dibujos.

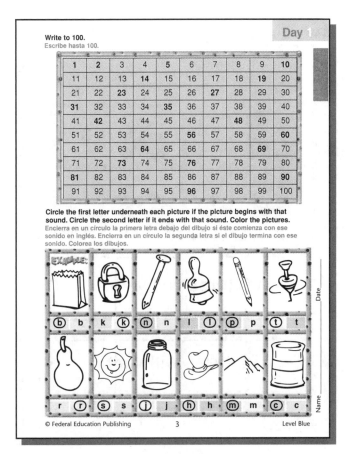

Date

Name

© Federal Education Publishing   3   Level Blue

Page 3

Write the capital letters of the alphabet.
Escribe el alfabeto en letra mayúscula.

EXAMPLE:
A B C D E F
G H I J K L M N O
P Q R S T U V W X Y
Z

Circle and write the correct word.
Encierra en un círculo y escribe la palabra correcta.

EXAMPLE:

1.	We will go in the ___van___.	(van)	can	ran
2.	I can help the ___man___.	mat	(man)	tan
3.	I am a good ___cook___.	book	moon	(cook)
4.	He is in his ___bed___.	red	(bed)	fan
5.	Can you get a ___book___?	the	it	(book)
6.	I am a ___sad___ man.	(sad)	glass	sled
7.	Find the big ___pig___.	tug	(pig)	pink
8.	Where is the ___flag___?	hid	run	(flag)
9.	I can run and ___jump___.	(jump)	cup	went
10.	I will take a hot ___bath___.	moth	(bath)	tooth

Level Blue   4   Bridges™

Page 4

Add or subtract.
Suma o resta.

3	4	5	2	0	8	1	7
+2	+3	+0	+1	+1	+1	+5	+2
5	7	5	3	1	9	6	9

	4	9	7	6	5	3	0	8
	-2	-3	-7	-4	-1	-2	-0	-5
	2	6	0	2	4	1	0	3

9	0	3	8	4	7	5	5
-4	+6	+5	+2	-3	-5	+5	-3
5	6	8	10	1	2	10	2

Circle the first letter in the box below each picture if the picture begins with that sound. Circle the second letter if the picture ends with that sound. Color the pictures.
Encierra en un círculo la primera letra debajo del dibujo si éste comienza con ese sonido en inglés. Encierra en un círculo la segunda letra si el dibujo termina con ese sonido. Colorea los dibujos.

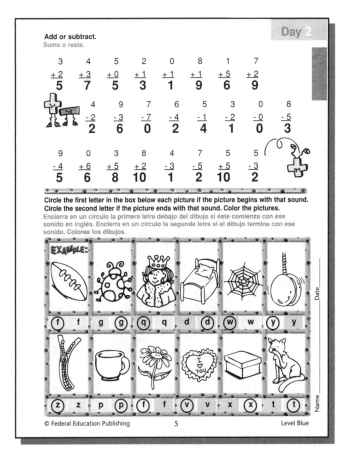

Date

Name

© Federal Education Publishing   5   Level Blue

Page 5

Write the lowercase letters of the alphabet.
Escribe el alfabeto en letra minúscula.

EXAMPLE:
a b c d e f
g h i j k l m n o p q r
s t u v w x y z

Practice reading these sentences. Draw a picture of your two favorite sentences.
Lee estas oraciones. Haz dibujos de tus oraciones favoritas.

1. The dog is stuck in the mud.
2. The cat will sit on Ann's lap.
3. The boy has a pet frog.
4. The man sat on his hat.
5. The hat is flat and smashed.
6. The rat ran on Sam's bed.
7. Sam is mad at the bad rat.
8. Fred met a girl with a wig.
9. The little bug bit the duck.
10. Fran had a pretty red dress.

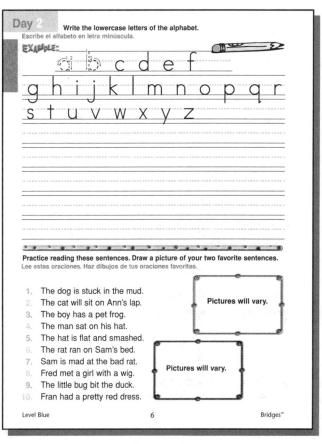

Pictures will vary.

Pictures will vary.

Level Blue   6   Bridges™

Page 6

© Federal Education Publishing   107   Level Blue

Page 7

Write the correct time on the small clocks. Draw hands on the big clocks.
Escribe la hora correcta en los relojes pequeños. Dibuja manecillas en los relojes grandes.

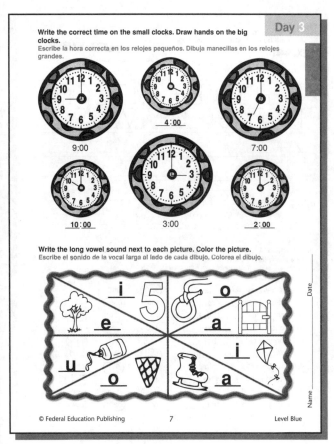

9:00   4:00   7:00

10:00   3:00   2:00

Write the long vowel sound next to each picture. Color the picture.
Escribe el sonido de la vocal larga al lado de cada dibujo. Colorea el dibujo.

i   5   o
e   a
u   i
o   a

© Federal Education Publishing   7   Level Blue

Page 7

Page 8

Match the sentence with the correct picture. Write the sentence number in the box.
Une la oración con el dibujo correcto. Escribe el número en el recuadro.

1. "Thank you for cleaning my yard!"
2. Dan and Trevor lick their ice cream.
3. The ice cream truck is coming.
4. The sun is very hot.

2   3
4   1

Draw and color pictures to go with these words.
Haz dibujos que coincidan con estas palabras.

Pictures will vary.

bug   log   bed   bib

Pictures will vary.

box   sit   rug   map

Level Blue   8   Bridges™

Page 8

Page 9

Complete the counting pattern.
Completa el patrón de números.

1 2 3

1 2 **3** **4** 5 6 7 **8** **9** 10 **11** **12**
13 14 **15** 16 **17** **18** 19 **20** 21 **22** **23** 24 **25**

31 **32** **33** 34 **35** 36 **37** **38** **39** 40 41 **42** **43**
44 **45** **46** 47 **48** **49** 50 **51** **52** 53 **54** **55** **56**

75 **76** 77 78 **79** **80** **81** 82 **83** 84 **85** **86** 87
88 **89** **90** **91** 92 **93** **94** **95** 96 **97** **98** **99** 100

Long and Short Vowels. Circle the correct word and color the picture.
Encierra la palabra correcta en un círculo y colorea el dibujo.

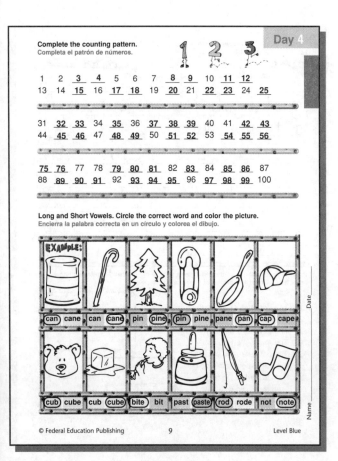

EXAMPLE:
(can) cane   can (cane)   pin (pine)   (pin) pine   pane (pan)   (cap) cape

(cub) cube   cub (cube)   bite (bit)   past (paste)   (rod) rode   not (note)

© Federal Education Publishing   9   Level Blue

Page 9

Page 10

Practice writing your first and last name.
Practica escribir tu nombre y tu apellido.

Answers will vary.

End each sentence with the correct punctuation mark: (.), (!), or (?).
Termina cada oración con el signo de puntuación correcto: (.), (!) o (?).

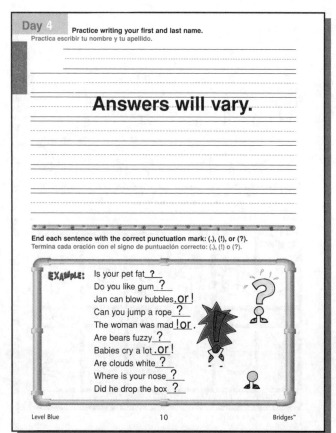

EXAMPLE: Is your pet fat _?_

Do you like gum _?_
Jan can blow bubbles. _or_ !
Can you jump a rope _?_
The woman was mad _!_ _or_ .
Are bears fuzzy _?_
Babies cry a lot. _or_ !
Are clouds white _?_
Where is your nose _?_
Did he drop the box _?_

Level Blue   10   Bridges™

Page 10

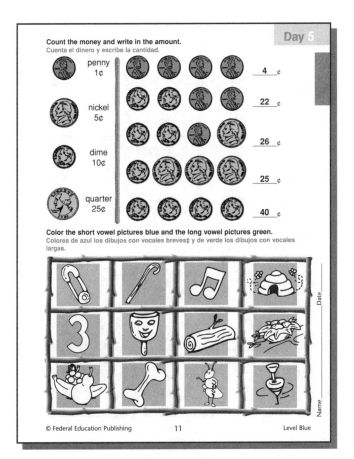

Page 11

Count the money and write in the amount.
Cuenta el dinero y escribe la cantidad.

penny 1¢

nickel 5¢

dime 10¢

quarter 25¢

4 ¢

22 ¢

26 ¢

25 ¢

40 ¢

Color the short vowel pictures blue and the long vowel pictures green.
Colorea de azul los dibujos con vocales breves‡ y de verde los dibujos con vocales largas.

© Federal Education Publishing   11   Level Blue

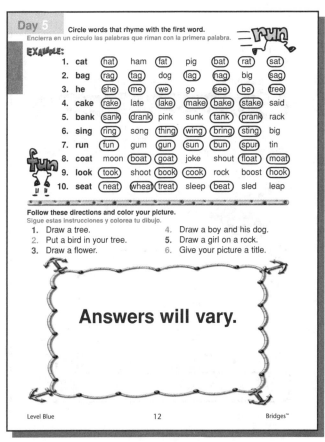

Page 12

Circle words that rhyme with the first word.
Encierra en un círculo las palabras que riman con la primera palabra.

EXAMPLE:

1. cat — (hat) ham (fat) pig (bat) (rat) (sat)
2. bag — (rag) (tag) dog (lag) (nag) big (sag)
3. he — (she) (me) (we) go (see) (be) (tree)
4. cake — (rake) late (lake) (make) (bake) (stake) said
5. bank — (sank) (drank) pink sunk (tank) (prank) rack
6. sing — (ring) song (thing) (wing) (bring) (sting) big
7. run — (fun) gum (gun) (sun) (bun) (spur) tin
8. coat — moon (boat) (goat) joke shout (float) (moat)
9. look — (took) shoot (book) (cook) rock boost (hook)
10. seat — (neat) (wheat) (treat) sleep (beat) sled leap

Follow these directions and color your picture.
Sigue estas instrucciones y colorea tu dibujo.

1. Draw a tree.
2. Put a bird in your tree.
3. Draw a flower.
4. Draw a boy and his dog.
5. Draw a girl on a rock.
6. Give your picture a title.

Answers will vary.

Level Blue   12   Bridges™

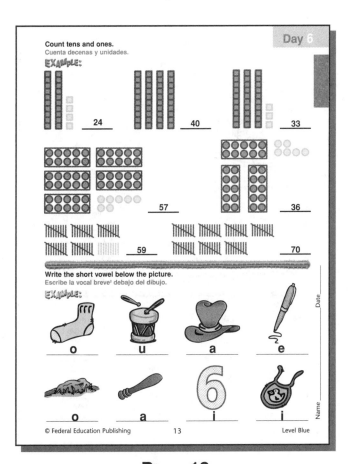

Page 13

Count tens and ones.
Cuenta decenas y unidades.

EXAMPLE:

24

40

33

57

36

59

70

Write the short vowel below the picture.
Escribe la vocal breve¹ debajo del dibujo.

EXAMPLE:

o   u   a   e

o   a   i   i

© Federal Education Publishing   13   Level Blue

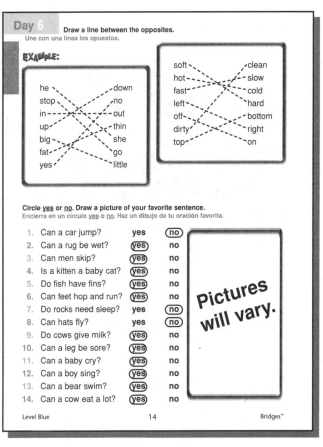

Page 14

Draw a line between the opposites.
Une con una línea los opuestos.

EXAMPLE:

he — down
stop — no
in — out
up — thin
big — she
fat — go
yes — little

soft — clean
hot — slow
fast — cold
left — hard
off — bottom
dirty — right
top — on

Circle yes or no. Draw a picture of your favorite sentence.
Encierra en un círculo yes o no. Haz un dibujo de tu oración favorita.

1. Can a car jump? — yes — (no)
2. Can a rug be wet? — (yes) — no
3. Can men skip? — (yes) — no
4. Is a kitten a baby cat? — (yes) — no
5. Do fish have fins? — (yes) — no
6. Can feet hop and run? — (yes) — no
7. Do rocks need sleep? — yes — (no)
8. Can hats fly? — yes — (no)
9. Do cows give milk? — (yes) — no
10. Can a leg be sore? — (yes) — no
11. Can a baby cry? — (yes) — no
12. Can a boy sing? — (yes) — no
13. Can a bear swim? — (yes) — no
14. Can a cow eat a lot? — (yes) — no

Pictures will vary.

Level Blue   14   Bridges™

Page 15

Read and answer these math problems.
Lee y resuelve estos problemas de matemáticas.

1. Griffin has two green cars and eight red cars in his train. How many cars does Griffin have in all?

___2___ green cars   ___8___ red cars   ___10___ cars in train

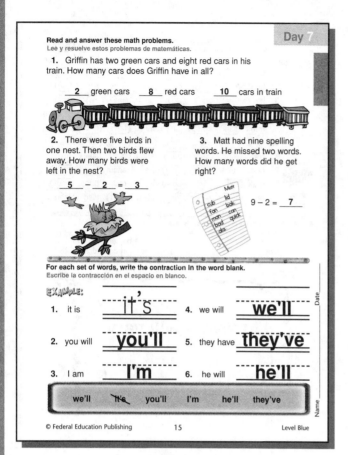

2. There were five birds in one nest. Then two birds flew away. How many birds were left in the nest?

___5___ − ___2___ = ___3___

3. Matt had nine spelling words. He missed two words. How many words did he get right?

9 − 2 = ___7___

For each set of words, write the contraction in the word blank.
Escribe la contracción en el espacio en blanco.

EXAMPLE:

1. it is   **it's**
2. you will   **you'll**
3. I am   **I'm**
4. we will   **we'll**
5. they have **they've**
6. he will   **he'll**

| we'll | it's | you'll | I'm | he'll | they've |

© Federal Education Publishing   15   Level Blue

Page 16

Draw a picture the color of the word.
Haz un dibujo del color de la palabra.

| blue | black | green |
| yellow | purple | red |

Answers will vary.

Circle the right word.
Encierra en un círculo la palabra correcta.

1. boy / (bone) / can
2. bunny / egg / (eye)
3. (sun) / sand / snake
4. fish / (frog) / fan
5. yellow / cow / (cat)
6. (book) / baby / boat
7. (six) / sat / one
8. wish / (fish) / shop
9. (rabbit) / mice / dog

Level Blue   16   Bridges™

Page 17

Count the money and write in the amount.
Cuenta el dinero y escribe la cantidad.

EXAMPLE:

1. 18 ¢
2. 13 ¢
3. 12 ¢
4. 17 ¢
5. 24 ¢
6. 37 ¢

Write and finish this sentence in three different ways.
Escribe y termina esta oración de tres formas distintas.

"I liked first grade because…"

1. _____
2. _____
3. _____

Answers will vary.

© Federal Education Publishing   17   Level Blue

Page 18

In each sentence, draw a circle around the two words that rhyme.
En cada oración, encierra en un círculo las dos palabras que riman.
Color the picture.
Colorea el dibujo.

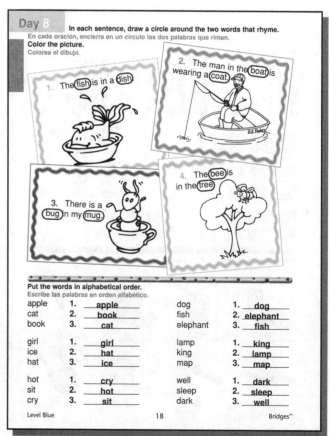

1. The (fish) is in a (dish).
2. The man in the (boat) is wearing a (coat).
3. There is a (bug) in my (mug).
4. The (bee) is in the (tree).

Put the words in alphabetical order.
Escribe las palabras en orden alfabético.

apple	1.	**apple**		dog	1.	**dog**
cat	2.	**book**		fish	2.	**elephant**
book	3.	**cat**		elephant	3.	**fish**

girl	1.	**girl**		lamp	1.	**king**
ice	2.	**hat**		king	2.	**lamp**
hat	3.	**ice**		map	3.	**map**

hot	1.	**cry**		well	1.	**dark**
sit	2.	**hot**		sleep	2.	**sleep**
cry	3.	**sit**		dark	3.	**well**

Level Blue   18   Bridges™

Page 19

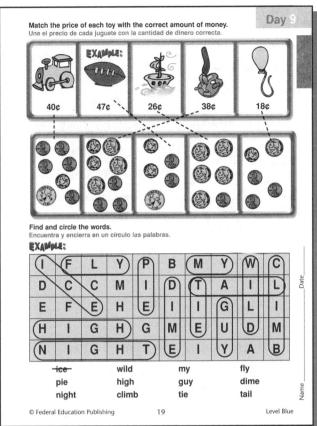

Day 9

Match the price of each toy with the correct amount of money.
Une el precio de cada juguete con la cantidad de dinero correcta.

EXAMPLE:

40¢   47¢   26¢   38¢   18¢

Find and circle the words.
Encuentra y encierra en un círculo las palabras.

EXAMPLE:

I	F	L	Y	P	B	M	Y	W	C
D	C	C	M	I	D	T	A	I	L
E	F	E	H	E	I	I	G	L	L
H	I	G	H	G	M	E	U	D	M
N	I	G	H	T	E	I	Y	A	B

~~ice~~   wild   my   fly

pie   high   guy   dime

night   climb   tie   tail

© Federal Education Publishing   19   Level Blue

Page 20

Day 9

Write the color words that fit in the boxes.
Escribe los nombres de los colores en los recuadros que corresponde.

yellow   orange   blue   black   purple
green   brown   red   gray   pink   white

EXAMPLE:

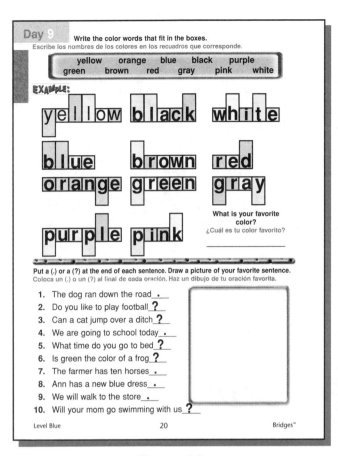

yellow   black   white
blue   brown   red
orange   green   gray

purple   pink

What is your favorite color?
¿Cuál es tu color favorito?
_____

Put a (.) or a (?) at the end of each sentence. Draw a picture of your favorite sentence.
Coloca un (.) o un (?) al final de cada oración. Haz un dibujo de tu oración favorita.

1. The dog ran down the road **.**
2. Do you like to play football **?**
3. Can a cat jump over a ditch **?**
4. We are going to school today **.**
5. What time do you go to bed **?**
6. Is green the color of a frog **?**
7. The farmer has ten horses **.**
8. Ann has a new blue dress **.**
9. We will walk to the store **.**
10. Will your mom go swimming with us **?**

Level Blue   20   Bridges™

Page 21

Day 10

Add or subtract.
Suma o resta.

5 + 6 = __11__	6 + 4 = __10__	3 + 8 = __11__
7 + 3 = __10__	9 - 5 = __4__	6 - 4 = __2__
10 + 1 = __11__	8 - 3 = __5__	2 + 9 = __11__
8 - 2 = __6__	10 - 4 = __6__	9 - 3 = __6__
10 - 5 = __5__	8 + 2 = __10__	9 + 3 = __12__
6 + 5 = __11__	7 + 4 = __11__	8 + 0 = __8__

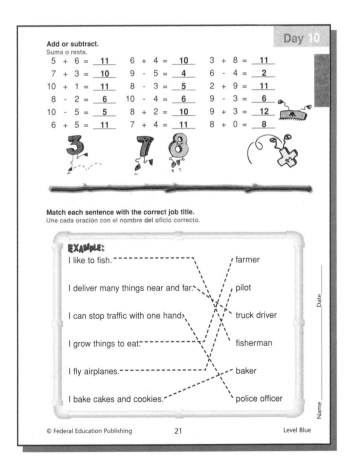

Match each sentence with the correct job title.
Une cada oración con el nombre del oficio correcto.

EXAMPLE:

I like to fish. ----- farmer

I deliver many things near and far. ----- pilot

I can stop traffic with one hand. ----- truck driver

I grow things to eat. ----- fisherman

I fly airplanes. ----- baker

I bake cakes and cookies. ----- police officer

© Federal Education Publishing   21   Level Blue

Page 22

Day 10

Find the hidden picture. Color the long i (ī) words blue and the short i (ĭ) words green. (The sound of (ī) can be in words with the letter y, too.)
Colorea las palabras con i larga‡ (i) de azul y las palabras con i breve‡ (i) de verde.

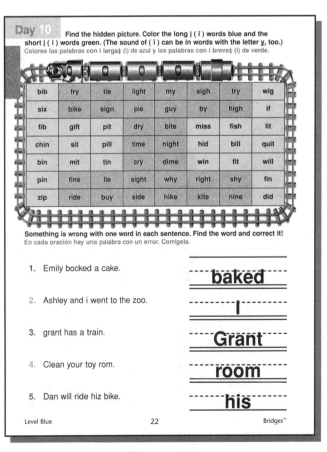

bib	fry	tie	light	my	sigh	try	wig
six	bike	sign	pie	guy	by	high	if
fib	gift	pit	dry	bite	miss	fish	lit
chin	sit	pill	time	night	hid	bill	quit
bin	mit	tin	cry	dime	win	fit	will
pin	fine	lie	sight	why	right	shy	fin
zip	ride	buy	side	hike	kite	nine	did

Something is wrong with one word in each sentence. Find the word and correct it!
En cada oración hay una palabra con un error. Corrígela.

1. Emily bocked a cake.   **baked**

2. Ashley and i went to the zoo.   **I**

3. grant has a train.   **Grant**

4. Clean your toy rom.   **room**

5. Dan will ride hiz bike.   **his**

Level Blue   22   Bridges™

Page 23

Page 23

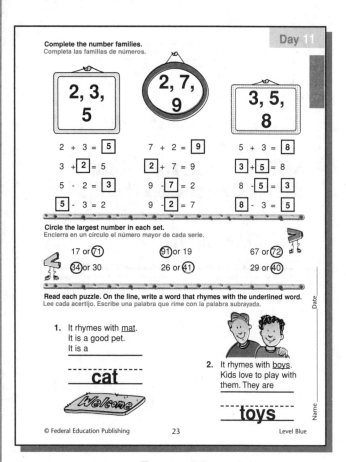

Complete the number families.
Completa las familias de números.

2, 3, 5   **2, 7, 9**   **3, 5, 8**

2 + 3 = **5**   7 + 2 = **9**   5 + 3 = **8**

3 + **2** = 5   **2** + 7 = 9   **3** + **5** = 8

5 − 2 = **3**   9 − **7** = 2   8 − **5** = **3**

5 − 3 = 2   9 − **2** = 7   **8** − 3 = **5**

Circle the largest number in each set.
Encierra en un círculo el número mayor de cada serie.

17 or (71)   (91) or 19   67 or (72)

(34) or 30   26 or (41)   29 or (40)

Read each puzzle. On the line, write a word that rhymes with the underlined word.
Lee cada acertijo. Escribe una palabra que rime con la palabra subrayada.

1. It rhymes with <u>mat</u>.
   It is a good pet.
   It is a

   cat

   Welcome

2. It rhymes with <u>boys</u>.
   Kids love to play with
   them. They are

   toys

© Federal Education Publishing   23   Level Blue

Page 24

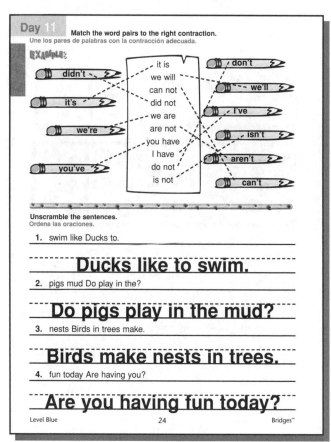

Match the word pairs to the right contraction.
Une los pares de palabras con la contracción adecuada.

EXAMPLE:

didn't   it is   don't
it's   we will   we'll
we're   can not   I've
you've   did not   isn't
   we are   aren't
   are not   can't
   you have
   I have
   do not
   is not

Unscramble the sentences.
Ordena las oraciones.

1. swim like Ducks to.

   Ducks like to swim.

2. pigs mud Do play in the?

   Do pigs play in the mud?

3. nests Birds in trees make.

   Birds make nests in trees.

4. fun today Are having you?

   Are you having fun today?

Level Blue   24   Bridges™

Page 25

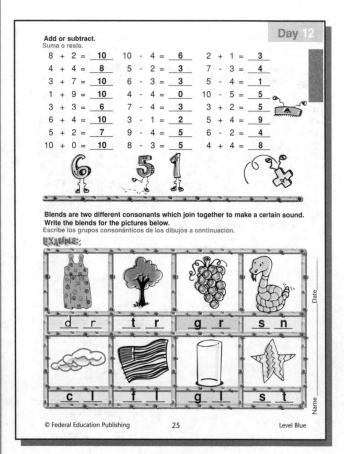

Add or subtract.
Suma o resta.

8 + 2 = **10**   10 − 4 = **6**   2 + 1 = **3**

4 + 4 = **8**   5 − 2 = **3**   7 − 3 = **4**

3 + 7 = **10**   6 − 3 = **3**   5 − 4 = **1**

1 + 9 = **10**   4 − 4 = **0**   10 − 5 = **5**

3 + 3 = **6**   7 − 4 = **3**   3 + 2 = **5**

6 + 4 = **10**   3 − 1 = **2**   5 + 4 = **9**

5 + 2 = **7**   9 − 4 = **5**   6 − 2 = **4**

10 + 0 = **10**   8 − 3 = **5**   4 + 4 = **8**

Blends are two different consonants which join together to make a certain sound. Write the blends for the pictures below.
Escribe los grupos consonánticos de los dibujos a continuación.

EXAMPLE:

d r   **t** r   **g** r   **s** n

c l   **f** l   **g** l   **s** t

© Federal Education Publishing   25   Level Blue

Page 26

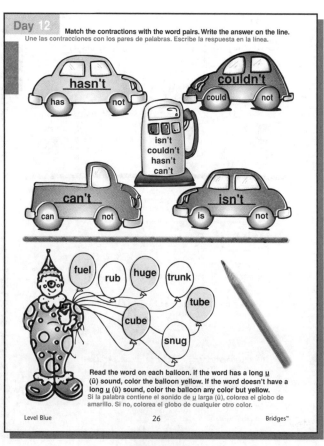

Match the contractions with the word pairs. Write the answer on the line.
Une las contracciones con los pares de palabras. Escribe la respuesta en la línea.

hasn't — has / not
couldn't — could / not

isn't
couldn't
hasn't
can't

can't — can / not
isn't — is / not

fuel   rub   huge   trunk
cube   tube
snug

Read the word on each balloon. If the word has a long u (ū) sound, color the balloon yellow. If the word doesn't have a long u (ū) sound, color the balloon any color but yellow.
Si la palabra contiene el sonido de u larga (ū), colorea el globo de amarillo. Si no, colorea el globo de cualquier otro color.

Level Blue   26   Bridges™

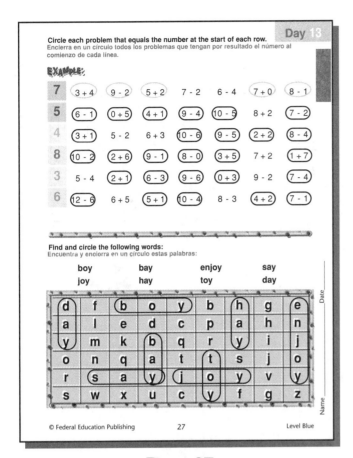

Page 27

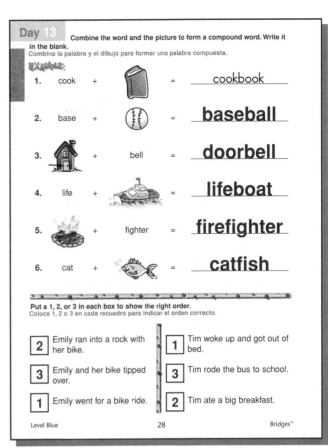

Page 28

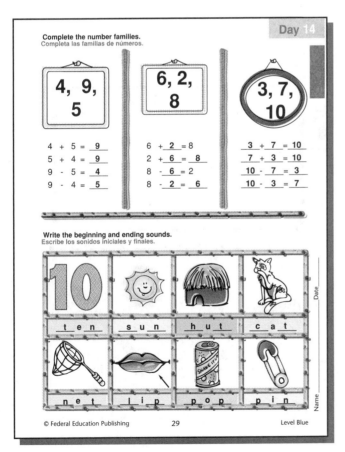

Page 29

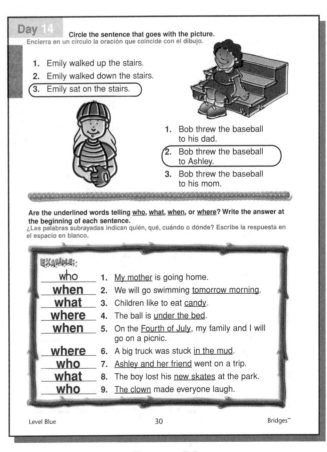

Page 30

Page 31

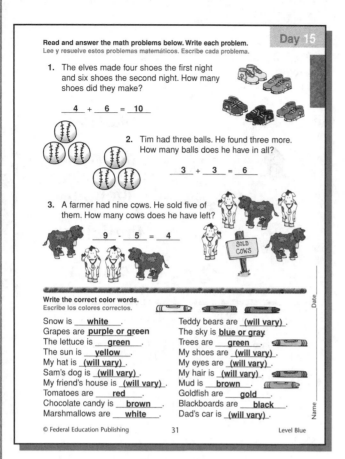

Read and answer the math problems below. Write each problem.
Lee y resuelve estos problemas matemáticos. Escribe cada problema.

1. The elves made four shoes the first night and six shoes the second night. How many shoes did they make?

$$\underline{\ 4\ } + \underline{\ 6\ } = \underline{\ 10\ }$$

2. Tim had three balls. He found three more. How many balls does he have in all?

$$\underline{\ 3\ } + \underline{\ 3\ } = \underline{\ 6\ }$$

3. A farmer had nine cows. He sold five of them. How many cows does he have left?

$$\underline{\ 9\ } - \underline{\ 5\ } = \underline{\ 4\ }$$

SOLD COWS

Write the correct color words.
Escribe los colores correctos.

Snow is __white__ .
Grapes are __purple or green__ .
The lettuce is __green__ .
The sun is __yellow__ .
My hat is __(will vary)__ .
Sam's dog is __(will vary)__ .
My friend's house is __(will vary)__ .
Tomatoes are __red__ .
Chocolate candy is __brown__ .
Marshmallows are __white__ .

Teddy bears are __(will vary)__ .
The sky is __blue or gray__ .
Trees are __green__ .
My shoes are __(will vary)__ .
My eyes are __(will vary)__ .
My hair is __(will vary)__ .
Mud is __brown__ .
Goldfish are __gold__ .
Blackboards are __black__ .
Dad's car is __(will vary)__ .

Date

Name

© Federal Education Publishing   31   Level Blue

Page 32

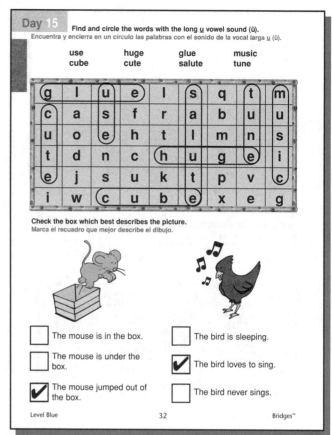

Find and circle the words with the long u vowel sound (ü).
Encuentra y encierra en un círculo las palabras con el sonido de la vocal larga u (ü).

use	huge	glue	music
cube	cute	salute	tune

g	l	u	e	l	s	q	t	m
c	a	s	f	r	a	b	u	u
u	o	e	h	t	l	m	n	s
t	d	n	c	h	u	g	e	i
e	j	s	u	k	t	p	v	c
i	w	c	u	b	e	x	e	g

Check the box which best describes the picture.
Marca el recuadro que mejor describe el dibujo.

☐ The mouse is in the box.

☐ The mouse is under the box.

☑ The mouse jumped out of the box.

☐ The bird is sleeping.

☑ The bird loves to sing.

☐ The bird never sings.

Level Blue   32   Bridges™

Page 35

Complete the counting patterns.
Completa las series.

10	**20**	30	**40**	50	60	**70**	80	90	**100**

5	**10**	**15**	20	25	30	**35**	**40**	45	50
55	60	65	**70**	75	80	85	**90**	95	100

2	**4**	6	**8**	10	**12**	14	16	**18**	20	**22**
24	**26**	28	30	32	34	**36**	38	40	**42**	44

Write in the short and long vowels.
Escribe las vocales breves¹ y largas.

EXAMPLE:

r _a_ ke	t _u_ be	b _o_ x	d _u_ ck
t _i_ re	l _a_ mp	m _i_ lk	t _o_ e

Date

Name

© Federal Education Publishing   35   Level Blue

Page 36

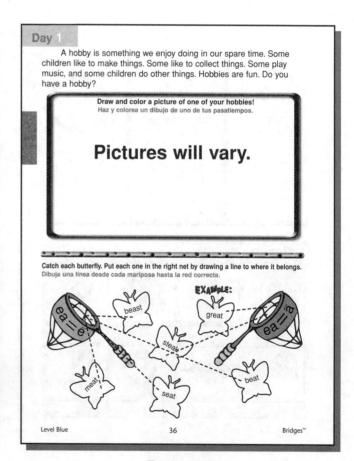

A hobby is something we enjoy doing in our spare time. Some children like to make things. Some like to collect things. Some play music, and some children do other things. Hobbies are fun. Do you have a hobby?

Draw and color a picture of one of your hobbies!
Haz y colorea un dibujo de uno de tus pasatiempos.

Pictures will vary.

Catch each butterfly. Put each one in the right net by drawing a line to where it belongs.
Dibuja una línea desde cada mariposa hasta la red correcta.

EXAMPLE:

ea = ē   beast   great   ea = ā

steal   meat   beat   seat

Level Blue   36   Bridges™

Page 37

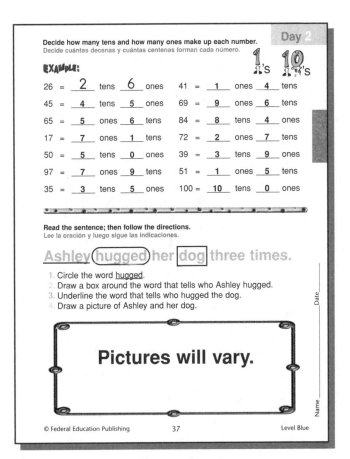

Decide how many tens and how many ones make up each number.
Decide cuántas decenas y cuántas centenas forman cada número.

1's 10's

EXAMPLE:

26 = **2** tens **6** ones   41 = **1** ones **4** tens

45 = **4** tens **5** ones   69 = **9** ones **6** tens

65 = **5** ones **6** tens   84 = **8** tens **4** ones

17 = **7** ones **1** tens   72 = **2** tens **7** ones

50 = **5** tens **0** ones   39 = **3** tens **9** ones

97 = **7** ones **9** tens   51 = **1** ones **5** tens

35 = **3** tens **5** ones   100 = **10** tens **0** ones

Read the sentence; then follow the directions.
Lee la oración y luego sigue las indicaciones.

Ashley (hugged) her [dog] three times.

1. Circle the word hugged.
2. Draw a box around the word that tells who Ashley hugged.
3. Underline the word that tells who hugged the dog.
4. Draw a picture of Ashley and her dog.

Pictures will vary.

© Federal Education Publishing   37   Level Blue

Page 38

Number these sentences in the order they happened.
Enumera estas oraciones en el orden en que sucedieron.

5 The sun came out. It was a pretty day.

2 The thunder roared, and the lightning flashed.

3 It rained and rained.

6 Emily put her umbrella away.

4 Emily walked under her umbrella.

1 The clouds came, and the sky was dark.

Finish the story.
Termina la historia.
Once there was a sun. The happy sun loved to shine its bright rays onto the earth because...

Answers will vary.

Level Blue   38   Bridges™

Page 39

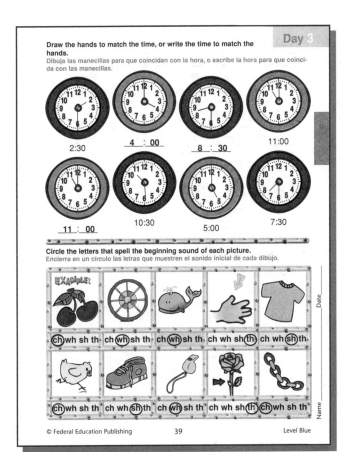

Draw the hands to match the time, or write the time to match the hands.
Dibuja las manecillas para que coincidan con la hora, o escribe la hora para que coincida con las manecillas.

2:30   **4** : **00**   **8** : **30**   11:00

11 : **00**   10:30   5:00   7:30

Circle the letters that spell the beginning sound of each picture.
Encierra en un círculo las letras que muestren el sonido inicial de cada dibujo.

EXAMPLE:

(ch) wh sh th   ch (wh) sh th   ch (wh) sh th   ch wh sh (th)   ch wh (sh) th

(ch) wh sh th   ch wh (sh) th   ch (wh) sh th   ch wh sh (th)   (ch) wh sh th

© Federal Education Publishing   39   Level Blue

Page 40

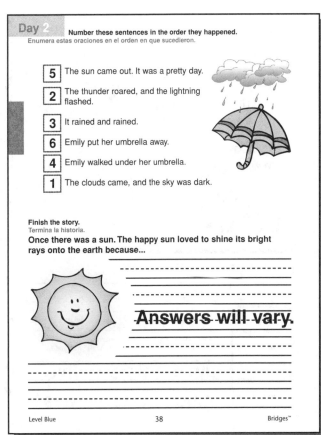

Read and decide.
Lee y decide qué encontró el hombre.

One day, a man went on a hunt. He hunted for a long time. At the end of the day, he was very happy. What do you think the man found? Did he find something to eat? Did he find something pretty? Did he find something funny? Decide what the man found and draw a picture of it!

Pictures will vary.

Put the following words in alphabetical order.
Escribe las siguientes palabras en orden alfabético.

he
up
fat
little
big
stop
and
out
slow
go

1. **and**   6. **little**
2. **big**   7. **out**
3. **fat**   8. **slow**
4. **go**   9. **stop**
5. **he**   10. **up**

Level Blue   40   Bridges™

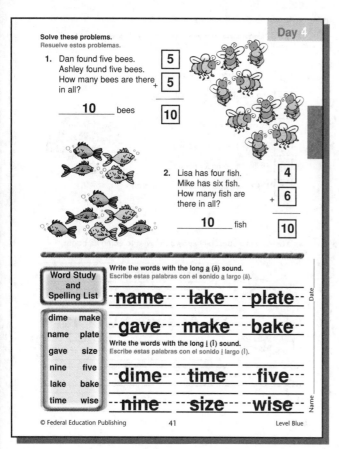

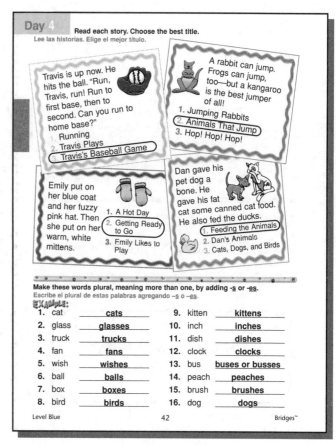

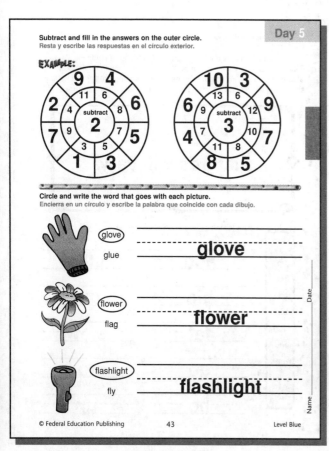

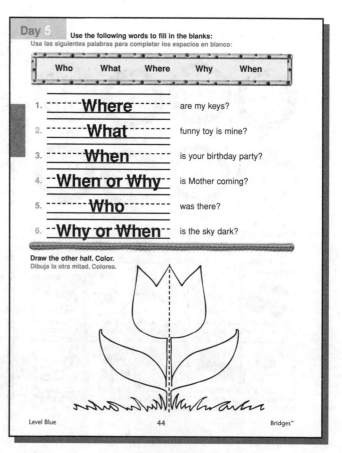

Page 41

Solve these problems.
Resuelve estos problemas.

1. Dan found five bees. Ashley found five bees. How many bees are there in all?

   5
   + 5
   10

   __10__ bees

2. Lisa has four fish. Mike has six fish. How many fish are there in all?

   4
   + 6
   10

   __10__ fish

Word Study and Spelling List

dime	make
name	plate
gave	size
nine	five
lake	bake
time	wise

Write the words with the long a (ā) sound.
Escribe estas palabras con el sonido a largo (ā).

name   lake   plate
gave   make   bake

Write the words with the long i (ī) sound.
Escribe estas palabras con el sonido i largo (ī).

dime   time   five
nine   size   wise

© Federal Education Publishing   41   Level Blue

Page 42

Read each story. Choose the best title.
Lee las historias. Elige el mejor título.

Travis is up now. He hits the ball. "Run, Travis, run! Run to first base, then to second. Can you run to home base?"
1. Running
2. Travis Plays
3. Travis's Baseball Game

A rabbit can jump. Frogs can jump, too—but a kangaroo is the best jumper of all!
1. Jumping Rabbits
2. Animals That Jump
3. Hop! Hop! Hop!

Emily put on her blue coat and her fuzzy pink hat. Then she put on her warm, white mittens.
1. A Hot Day
2. Getting Ready to Go
3. Emily Likes to Play

Dan gave his pet dog a bone. He gave his fat cat some canned cat food. He also fed the ducks.
1. Feeding the Animals
2. Dan's Animals
3. Cats, Dogs, and Birds

Make these words plural, meaning more than one, by adding -s or -es.
Escribe el plural de estas palabras agregando –s o –es.

EXAMPLE:

1.	cat	cats	9.	kitten	kittens
2.	glass	glasses	10.	inch	inches
3.	truck	trucks	11.	dish	dishes
4.	fan	fans	12.	clock	clocks
5.	wish	wishes	13.	bus	buses or busses
6.	ball	balls	14.	peach	peaches
7.	box	boxes	15.	brush	brushes
8.	bird	birds	16.	dog	dogs

Level Blue   42   Bridges™

Page 43

Subtract and fill in the answers on the outer circle.
Resta y escribe las respuestas en el círculo exterior.

EXAMPLE:

Circle and write the word that goes with each picture.
Encierra en un círculo y escribe la palabra que coincide con cada dibujo.

glove
glue
→ **glove**

flower
flag
→ **flower**

flashlight
fly
→ **flashlight**

© Federal Education Publishing   43   Level Blue

Page 44

Use the following words to fill in the blanks:
Usa las siguientes palabras para completar los espacios en blanco:

Who	What	Where	Why	When

1. **Where** are my keys?
2. **What** funny toy is mine?
3. **When** is your birthday party?
4. **When or Why** is Mother coming?
5. **Who** was there?
6. **Why or When** is the sky dark?

Draw the other half. Color.
Dibuja la otra mitad. Colorea.

Level Blue   44   Bridges™

Page 45

Solve the following problems.
Resuelve los siguientes problemas.

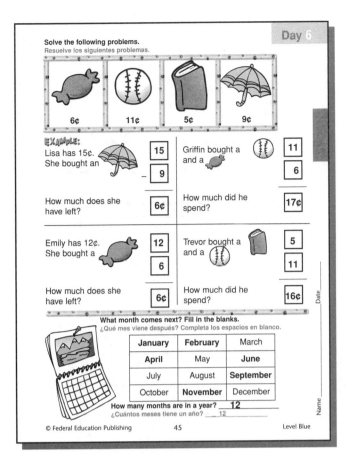

6¢	11¢	5¢	9¢

EXAMPLE:
Lisa has 15¢.
She bought an [umbrella]

15
− 9

How much does she have left? 6¢

Griffin bought a [baseball] and a [candy]

11
6

How much did he spend? 17¢

Emily has 12¢.
She bought a [candy]

12
6

How much does she have left? 6¢

Trevor bought a [book] and a [baseball]

5
11

How much did he spend? 16¢

What month comes next? Fill in the blanks.
¿Qué mes viene después? Completa los espacios en blanco.

January	February	March
April	May	**June**
July	August	**September**
October	**November**	December

How many months are in a year? **12**
¿Cuántos meses tiene un año? ___ 12

© Federal Education Publishing   45   Level Blue

Page 46

Write the correct word on each line.
Escribe la palabra correcta en cada línea.

1. Sam has a sore _____**throat**_____.
   thirst   throat   thunder

2. May I please have _____**three**_____ balls?
   three   third   fifth

3. My little _____**brother**_____ is three years old.
   mother   father   brother

4. We could walk _____**together**_____.
   together   rather   other

5. You need to _____**think**_____ fast.
   third   thank   think

Finish the story.
Termina la historia.

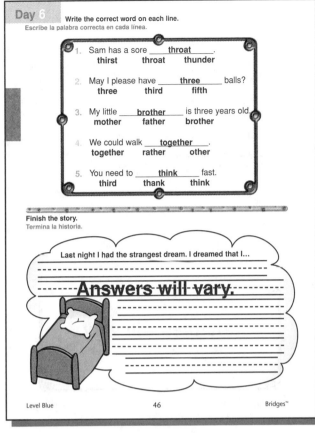

Last night I had the strangest dream. I dreamed that I...

~~Answers will vary.~~

Level Blue   46   Bridges™

Page 47

Do a survey with your family and friends to see which flavor of popsicle is the most popular.
Realiza una encuesta para determinar qué sabor de helado es la más popular.

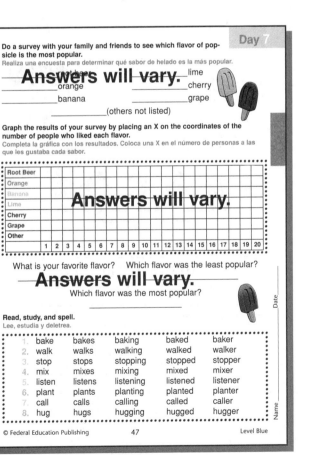

~~Answers will vary.~~
_____ root beer _____ lime
_____ orange _____ cherry
_____ banana _____ grape
_____ (others not listed)

Graph the results of your survey by placing an X on the coordinates of the number of people who liked each flavor.
Completa la gráfica con los resultados. Coloca una X en el número de personas a las que les gustaba cada sabor.

Root Beer																				
Orange																				
Banana																				
Lime																				
Cherry																				
Grape																				
Other	1	2	3	4	5	6	7	8	9	10	11	12	13	14	15	16	17	18	19	20

~~Answers will vary.~~

What is your favorite flavor?   Which flavor was the least popular?

~~Answers will vary.~~

Which flavor was the most popular?
_____

Read, study, and spell.
Lee, estudia y deletrea.

1.	bake	bakes	baking	baked	baker
2.	walk	walks	walking	walked	walker
3.	stop	stops	stopping	stopped	stopper
4.	mix	mixes	mixing	mixed	mixer
5.	listen	listens	listening	listened	listener
6.	plant	plants	planting	planted	planter
7.	call	calls	calling	called	caller
8.	hug	hugs	hugging	hugged	hugger

© Federal Education Publishing   47   Level Blue

Page 48

Read the story; then answer the questions below.
Lee la historia y luego contesta las preguntas.

Mike lives on a farm. He wakes up early to do chores. Mike feeds the horses and pigs. He also collects the eggs. Sometimes, he helps his dad milk the cows. His favorite thing to do in the morning is eat breakfast.

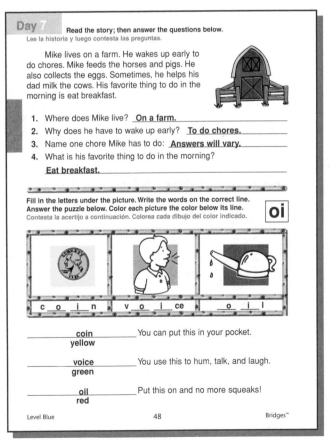

1. Where does Mike live? **On a farm.**
2. Why does he have to wake up early? **To do chores.**
3. Name one chore Mike has to do: **Answers will vary.**
4. What is his favorite thing to do in the morning?
   Eat breakfast.

Fill in the letters under the picture. Write the words on the correct line.
Answer the puzzle below. Color each picture the color below its line.
Contesta la acertijo a continuación. Colorea cada dibujo del color indicado.

oi

c o i n	v o i ce	o i l

_____**coin**_____   You can put this in your pocket.
yellow

_____**voice**_____   You use this to hum, talk, and laugh.
green

_____**oil**_____   Put this on and no more squeaks!
red

Level Blue   48   Bridges™

Add.
Suma.

1. 2   1   4   5   2   4   5   3   8
    2   1   4   5   3   3   4   5   0
   +2 +1 +4 +5 +2 +0 +5 +3 +2
   ___ ___ ___ ___ ___ ___ ___ ___ ___
    6   3   12 15   7   7   14 11 10

2. 3   6   7   10   8   5   9   2   4
    3   6   0   10   3   1   0   3   4
   +3 +6 +7 +10 +2 +5 +1 +7 +3
   ___ ___ ___ ___ ___ ___ ___ ___ ___
    9   18 14 30   13 11 10 12 11

Give some facts about you and your family. Draw a picture of your family.
Proporciona algunos detalles sobre ti y tu familia. Haz un dibujo de tu familia.

1. I live in __Answers will vary.__
2. I have _____ sisters.
3. I have _____ brothers.
4. My mom's name is _____
5. My dad's name is _____

6. This summer we are going to _____.
7. I am _____ years old.
8. We have a pet _____
9. My favorite food is _____
10. My favorite color is _____

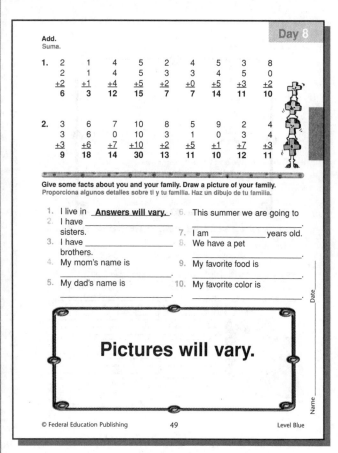

Pictures will vary.

Page 49

What day comes next? Fill in the blanks.
¿Qué día viene después? Completa los espacios en blanco.

Sunday, __Monday__, __Tuesday__, Wednesday, __Thursday__, Friday, and __Saturday__.

How many days are in a week? __7__

Name the days you go to school during the week.
__Monday__, __Tuesday__, __Wednesday__, __Thursday__, __Friday__

Complete these sentences by unscrambling the words and writing them in the blanks.
Ordena las palabras y escríbelas en los espacios en blanco.

1. Mike had a __gift__ for __his__ mother.
   igft   ihs

2. The __car__ has a broken window.
   acr

3. A bee __sat__ on __the__ flower.
   ats   hte

4. My __dad__ works at the __store__.
   add   tsoer

5. Sue __has__ a __pet__ dog named Spot.
   sha   ept

Page 50

Add.
Suma.

 5   8   3   9   15   10   8   9   6
+7   +4   +7   +5   +2   +6   +3   +4   +5
___ ___ ___ ___ ___ ___ ___ ___ ___
12   12   10   14   17   16   11   13   11

Subtract.
Resta.

12   9   11   8   10   6   7   12   10
-8   -4   -7   -8   -2   -2   -5   -4   -6
___ ___ ___ ___ ___ ___ ___ ___ ___
 4   5   4   0   8   4   2   8   4

Write the words that match the clues.
Escribe las palabras que coincidan con las pistas.

EXAMPLE:
1. It begins like <u>stuck</u>. It rhymes with <u>late</u>.
   __state__

2. It begins like <u>rip</u>. It rhymes with <u>cake</u>.
   __rake__

3. It begins like <u>very</u>. It rhymes with <u>note</u>. __vote__

4. It begins like <u>break</u>. It rhymes with <u>him</u>. __brim__

5. It begins like <u>gum</u>. It rhymes with <u>late</u>. __gate__

6. It begins like <u>trip</u>. It rhymes with <u>rim</u>. __trim__

Page 51

Read the story below and then answer the questions.
Lee la historia y luego contesta las preguntas.

Ashley has a box of peaches. She wants to take the peaches home to her mother, so her mother can make a peach pie. Ashley says, "I love to eat peach pie!"

1. Who has a box of peaches? __Ashley__
2. Whom does she want to take the peaches to? __her mother__
3. What does she want her mother to make? __peach pie__
4. Ashley says, "I love to eat __peach pie__!"

Complete the phrase below. Write at least three complete sentences.
Completa la frase a continuación. Escribe por lo menos tres oraciones completas.

I like myself because I can…

Answers will vary.

Page 52

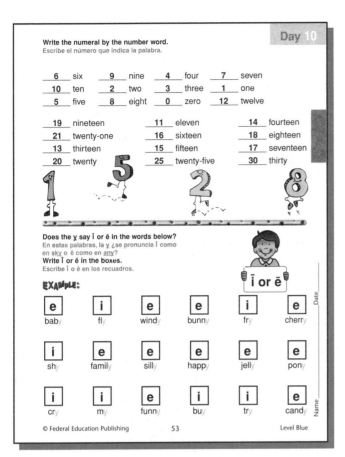

Page 53

Write the numeral by the number word.
Escribe el número que indica la palabra.

6	six	9	nine	4	four	7	seven
10	ten	2	two	3	three	1	one
5	five	8	eight	0	zero	12	twelve

19	nineteen	11	eleven	14	fourteen
21	twenty-one	16	sixteen	18	eighteen
13	thirteen	15	fifteen	17	seventeen
20	twenty	25	twenty-five	30	thirty

Does the y say ī or ē in the words below?
En estas palabras, la y ¿se pronuncia ī como en sky o ē como en any?
Write ī or ē in the boxes.
Escribe ī o ē en los recuadros.

ī or ē

EXAMPLE:

e	i	e	e	i	e
baby	fly	windy	bunny	fry	cherry

i	e	e	e	e	e
shy	family	silly	happy	jelly	pony

i	i	e	i	i	e
cry	my	funny	buy	try	candy

© Federal Education Publishing 53 Level Blue

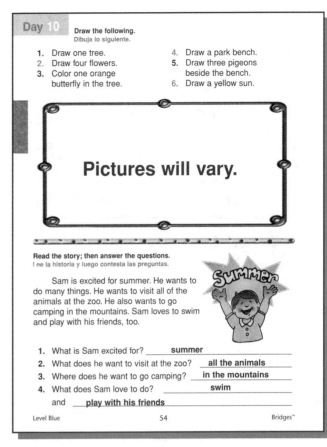

Page 54

Draw the following.
Dibuja lo siguiente.

1. Draw one tree.
2. Draw four flowers.
3. Color one orange butterfly in the tree.
4. Draw a park bench.
5. Draw three pigeons beside the bench.
6. Draw a yellow sun.

Pictures will vary.

Read the story; then answer the questions.
Lee la historia y luego contesta las preguntas.

Sam is excited for summer. He wants to do many things. He wants to visit all of the animals at the zoo. He also wants to go camping in the mountains. Sam loves to swim and play with his friends, too.

1. What is Sam excited for? **summer**
2. What does he want to visit at the zoo? **all the animals**
3. Where does he want to go camping? **in the mountains**
4. What does Sam love to do? **swim**
   and **play with his friends**

Level Blue 54 Bridges™

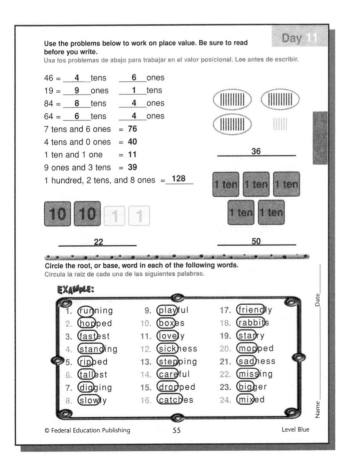

Page 55

Use the problems below to work on place value. Be sure to read before you write.
Usa los problemas de abajo para trabajar en el valor posicional. Lee antes de escribir.

46 = **4** tens **6** ones
19 = **9** ones **1** tens
84 = **8** tens **4** ones
64 = **6** tens **4** ones
7 tens and 6 ones = **76**
4 tens and 0 ones = **40**
1 ten and 1 one = **11**
9 ones and 3 tens = **39**
1 hundred, 2 tens, and 8 ones = **128**

36

1 ten 1 ten 1 ten

1 ten 1 ten

10 10 1 1

22   50

Circle the root, or base, word in each of the following words.
Circula la raíz de cada una de las siguientes palabras.

EXAMPLE:

1. running
2. hopped
3. fastest
4. standing
5. ripped
6. tallest
7. digging
8. slowly
9. playful
10. boxes
11. lovely
12. sickness
13. stepping
14. careful
15. dropped
16. catches
17. friendly
18. rabbits
19. starry
20. mopped
21. sadness
22. missing
23. bigger
24. mixed

© Federal Education Publishing 55 Level Blue

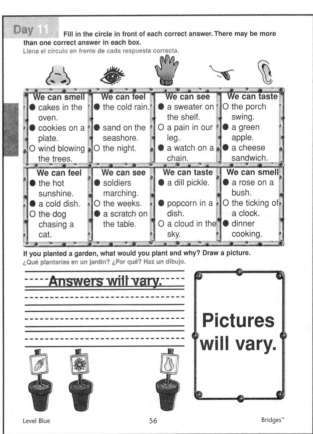

Page 56

Fill in the circle in front of each correct answer. There may be more than one correct answer in each box.
Llena el círculo en frente de cada respuesta correcta.

We can smell	We can feel	We can see	We can taste
● cakes in the oven.	● the cold rain.	● a sweater on the shelf.	○ the porch swing.
● cookies on a plate.	● sand on the seashore.	○ a pain in our leg.	● a green apple.
○ wind blowing the trees.	○ the night.	● a watch on a chain.	● a cheese sandwich.

We can feel	We can see	We can taste	We can smell
● the hot sunshine.	● soldiers marching.	● a dill pickle.	● a rose on a bush.
● a cold dish.	○ the weeks.	● popcorn in a dish.	○ the ticking of a clock.
○ the dog chasing a cat.	● a scratch on the table.	○ a cloud in the sky.	● dinner cooking.

If you planted a garden, what would you plant and why? Draw a picture.
¿Qué plantarías en un jardín? ¿Por qué? Haz un dibujo.

Answers will vary.

Pictures will vary.

Level Blue 56 Bridges™

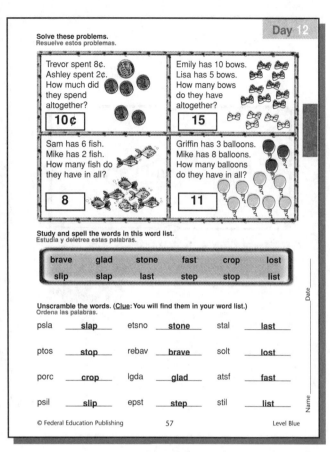

Page 57

Solve these problems.
Resuelve estos problemas.

Trevor spent 8¢.
Ashley spent 2¢.
How much did
they spend
altogether?

10¢

Emily has 10 bows.
Lisa has 5 bows.
How many bows
do they have
altogether?

15

Sam has 6 fish.
Mike has 2 fish.
How many fish do
they have in all?

8

Griffin has 3 balloons.
Mike has 8 balloons.
How many balloons
do they have in all?

11

Study and spell the words in this word list.
Estudia y deletrea estas palabras.

| brave | glad | stone | fast | crop | lost |
| slip | slap | last | step | stop | list |

Unscramble the words. (Clue: You will find them in your word list.)
Ordena las palabras.

psla **slap**   etsno **stone**   stal **last**

ptos **stop**   rebav **brave**   solt **lost**

porc **crop**   lgda **glad**   atsf **fast**

psil **slip**   epst **step**   stil **list**

© Federal Education Publishing   57   Level Blue

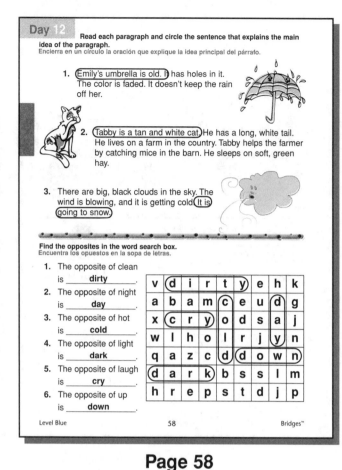

Page 58

Read each paragraph and circle the sentence that explains the main idea of the paragraph.
Encierra en un círculo la oración que explique la idea principal del párrafo.

1. (Emily's umbrella is old. It) has holes in it. The color is faded. It doesn't keep the rain off her.

2. (Tabby is a tan and white cat) He has a long, white tail. He lives on a farm in the country. Tabby helps the farmer by catching mice in the barn. He sleeps on soft, green hay.

3. There are big, black clouds in the sky. The wind is blowing, and it is getting cold (It is going to snow.)

Find the opposites in the word search box.
Encuentra los opuestos en la sopa de letras.

1. The opposite of clean is **dirty**
2. The opposite of night is **day**
3. The opposite of hot is **cold**
4. The opposite of light is **dark**
5. The opposite of laugh is **cry**
6. The opposite of up is **down**

v	d	i	r	t	y	e	h	k
a	b	a	m	c	e	u	d	g
x	c	r	y	o	d	s	a	j
w	l	h	o	l	r	j	y	n
q	a	z	c	d	d	o	w	n
d	a	r	k	b	s	s	l	m
h	r	e	p	s	t	d	j	p

Level Blue   58   Bridges™

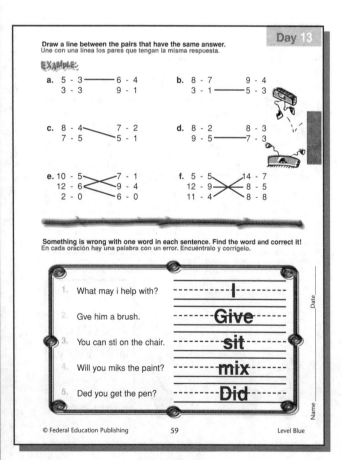

Page 59

Draw a line between the pairs that have the same answer.
Une con una línea los pares que tengan la misma respuesta.

EXAMPLE

a. 5 - 3 —— 6 - 4
   3 - 3 —— 9 - 1

b. 8 - 7   9 - 4
   3 - 1 —— 5 - 3

c. 8 - 4   7 - 2
   7 - 5   5 - 1

d. 8 - 2   8 - 3
   9 - 5   7 - 3

e. 10 - 5   7 - 1
   12 - 6   9 - 4
   2 - 0   6 - 0

f. 5 - 5   14 - 7
   12 - 9   8 - 5
   11 - 4   8 - 8

Something is wrong with one word in each sentence. Find the word and correct it!
En cada oración hay una palabra con un error. Encuéntralo y corrígelo.

1. What may i help with?   **I**

2. Gve him a brush.   **Give**

3. You can sti on the chair.   **sit**

4. Will you miks the paint?   **mix**

5. Ded you get the pen?   **Did**

© Federal Education Publishing   59   Level Blue

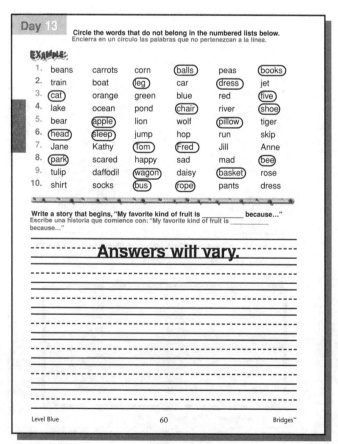

Page 60

Circle the words that do not belong in the numbered lists below.
Encierra en un círculo las palabras que no pertenezcan a la línea.

EXAMPLE

1. beans   carrots   corn   (balls)   peas   (books)
2. train   boat   (leg)   car   (dress)   jet
3. (cat)   orange   green   blue   red   (five)
4. lake   ocean   pond   (chair)   river   (shoe)
5. bear   (apple)   lion   wolf   (pillow)   tiger
6. (head)   (sleep)   jump   hop   run   skip
7. Jane   Kathy   (Tom)   (Fred)   Jill   Anne
8. (park)   scared   happy   sad   mad   (bee)
9. tulip   daffodil   (wagon)   daisy   (basket)   rose
10. shirt   socks   (bus)   (rope)   pants   dress

Write a story that begins, "My favorite kind of fruit is _____ because…"
Escribe una historia que comience con: "My favorite kind of fruit is _____ because…"

Answers will vary.

Level Blue   60   Bridges™

Page 61

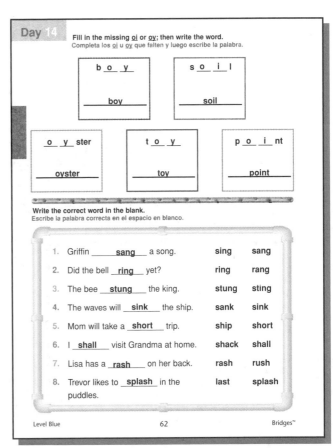

Page 62

Finish the chart.
Termina los siguientes patrones.

1. 2 4 6 8 10 12

2. 3 6 9 12 15 18

3. 4 8 12 16 20 24

4. 5 10 15 20 25 30

Use the Word Study List to do the following activity.
Usa la Lista de Estudio de Palabras para realizar esta actividad.

Word Study List

go
me
we
he
no
so
she
be
see
bee

1. Write the word go. Change the beginning letter to make two more words.

go   so   no

2. Write the words that mean the opposite of yes and stop.

no   go

3. Write she, then write two more words that end the same.

she   will vary   will vary

© Federal Education Publishing   63   Level Blue

Page 63

Fill in the blank with a homonym for the underlined word.
Remember: Homonyms sound the same but have different meanings.
Completa el espacio en blanco con un homónimo de la palabra subrayada.

| made | new | ~~eight~~ | sea | through |
| wood | right | bee | hear | knot |

EXAMPLE:

1. Ashley ate _____ **eight** _____ pancakes for breakfast.
2. Stay here and you can _____ **hear** _____ the music.
3. Can you see the _____ **sea** _____ from the top of the hill?
4. Be careful when you catch a _____ **bee** _____ .
5. Would you get some _____ **wood** _____ for the fire?
6. Did you write the _____ **right** _____ answer?
7. He threw the ball _____ **through** _____ the window.
8. Our maid _____ **made** _____ all the beds.
9. The little girl could not tie a _____ **knot** _____ in the rope.
10. My mother knew the _____ **new** _____ teacher.

What did you do yesterday? Write down your activities in the order you did them.
Escribe lo que hiciste ayer en el orden en que lo hiciste.

1. _____
2. _____
3. _____
4. _____
5. _____
6. _____

Answers will vary.

Level Blue   64   Bridges™

Page 64

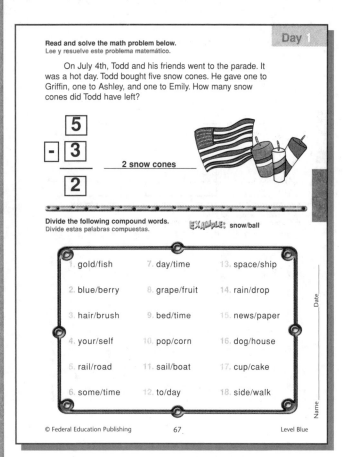

Read and solve the math problem below.
Lee y resuelve este problema matemático.

Day 1

On July 4th, Todd and his friends went to the parade. It was a hot day. Todd bought five snow cones. He gave one to Griffin, one to Ashley, and one to Emily. How many snow cones did Todd have left?

$$\begin{array}{r} 5 \\ -\ 3 \\ \hline 2 \end{array}$$ _____ 2 snow cones

Divide the following compound words.
Divide estas palabras compuestas.

EXAMPLE: snow/ball

1. gold/fish
2. blue/berry
3. hair/brush
4. your/self
5. rail/road
6. some/time
7. day/time
8. grape/fruit
9. bed/time
10. pop/corn
11. sail/boat
12. to/day
13. space/ship
14. rain/drop
15. news/paper
16. dog/house
17. cup/cake
18. side/walk

Page 67

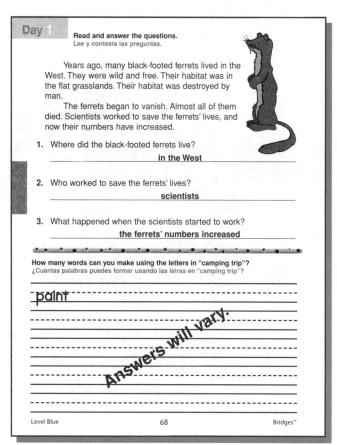

Day 1

Read and answer the questions.
Lee y contesta las preguntas.

Years ago, many black-footed ferrets lived in the West. They were wild and free. Their habitat was in the flat grasslands. Their habitat was destroyed by man.

The ferrets began to vanish. Almost all of them died. Scientists worked to save the ferrets' lives, and now their numbers have increased.

1. Where did the black-footed ferrets live?
   in the West

2. Who worked to save the ferrets' lives?
   scientists

3. What happened when the scientists started to work?
   the ferrets' numbers increased

How many words can you make using the letters in "camping trip"?
¿Cuántas palabras puedes formar usando las letras en "camping trip"?

paint

Answers will vary.

Page 68

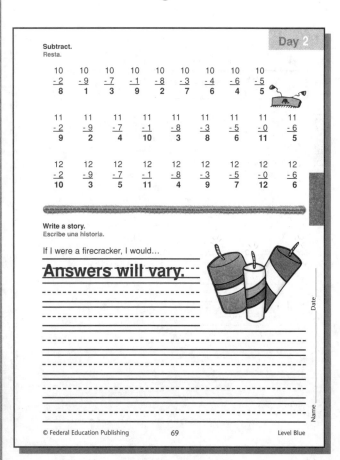

Day 2

Subtract.
Resta.

10	10	10	10	10	10	10	10	10
-2	-9	-7	-1	-8	-3	-4	-6	-5
8	1	3	9	2	7	6	4	5

11	11	11	11	11	11	11	11	11
-2	-9	-7	-1	-8	-3	-5	-0	-6
9	2	4	10	3	8	6	11	5

12	12	12	12	12	12	12	12	12
-2	-9	-7	-1	-8	-3	-5	-0	-6
10	3	5	11	4	9	7	12	6

Write a story.
Escribe una historia.

If I were a firecracker, I would…

Answers will vary.

Page 69

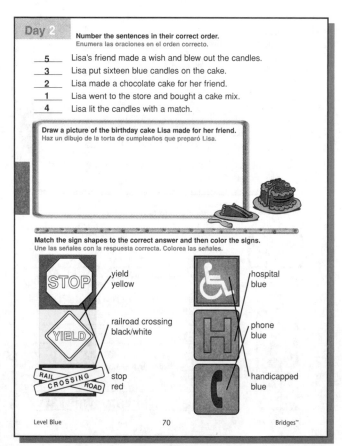

Day 2

Number the sentences in their correct order.
Enumera las oraciones en el orden correcto.

5 — Lisa's friend made a wish and blew out the candles.
3 — Lisa put sixteen blue candles on the cake.
2 — Lisa made a chocolate cake for her friend.
1 — Lisa went to the store and bought a cake mix.
4 — Lisa lit the candles with a match.

Draw a picture of the birthday cake Lisa made for her friend.
Haz un dibujo de la torta de cumpleaños que preparó Lisa.

Match the sign shapes to the correct answer and then color the signs.
Une las señales con la respuesta correcta. Colorea las señales.

STOP — yield / yellow

YIELD — railroad crossing / black/white

RAIL CROSSING ROAD — stop / red

— hospital / blue

H — phone / blue

— handicapped / blue

Page 70

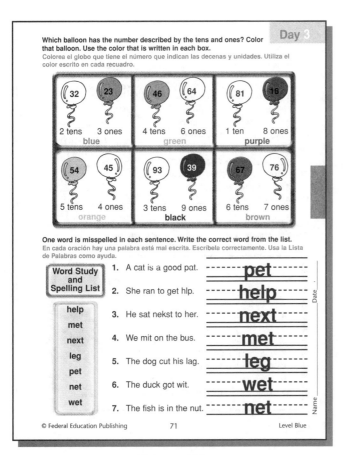

Which balloon has the number described by the tens and ones? Color that balloon. Use the color that is written in each box.
Colorea el globo que tiene el número que indican las decenas y unidades. Utiliza el color escrito en cada recuadro.

32	23	46	64	81	18
2 tens 3 ones		4 tens 6 ones		1 ten 8 ones	
blue		green		purple	

54	45	93	39	67	76
5 tens 4 ones		3 tens 9 ones		6 tens 7 ones	
orange		black		brown	

One word is misspelled in each sentence. Write the correct word from the list.
En cada oración hay una palabra está mal escrita. Escríbela correctamente. Usa la Lista de Palabras como ayuda.

Word Study and Spelling List

help
met
next
leg
pet
net
wet

1. A cat is a good pat. **pet**
2. She ran to get hlp. **help**
3. He sat nekst to her. **next**
4. We mit on the bus. **met**
5. The dog cut his lag. **leg**
6. The duck got wit. **wet**
7. The fish is in the nut. **net**

© Federal Education Publishing   71   Level Blue

Page 71

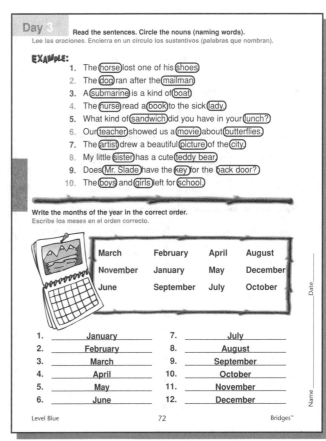

Read the sentences. Circle the nouns (naming words).
Lee las oraciones. Encierra en un círculo los sustantivos (palabras que nombran).

EXAMPLE:
1. The (horse) lost one of his (shoes)
2. The (dog) ran after the (mailman)
3. A (submarine) is a kind of (boat)
4. The (nurse) read a (book) to the sick (lady).
5. What kind of (sandwich) did you have in your (lunch?)
6. Our (teacher) showed us a (movie) about (butterflies).
7. The (artist) drew a beautiful (picture) of the (city).
8. My little (sister) has a cute (teddy bear)
9. Does (Mr. Slade) have the (key) for the (back door?)
10. The (boys) and (girls) left for (school).

Write the months of the year in the correct order.
Escribe los meses en el orden correcto.

March	February	April	August
November	January	May	December
June	September	July	October

1. January
2. February
3. March
4. April
5. May
6. June
7. July
8. August
9. September
10. October
11. November
12. December

Level Blue   72   Bridges™

Page 72

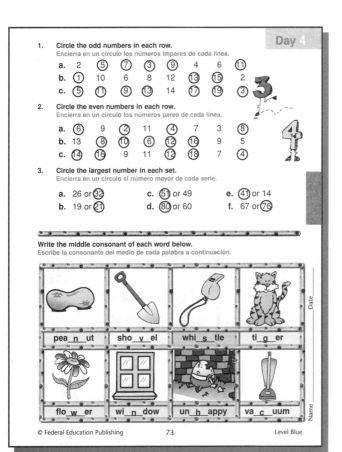

1. Circle the odd numbers in each row.
   Encierra en un círculo los números impares de cada línea.
   a. 2 (5) (7) (3) (9) 4 6 (11)
   b. (1) 10 6 8 12 (13) (15) 2
   c. (5) (11) (9) (13) 14 (17) (19) (3)

2. Circle the even numbers in each row.
   Encierra en un círculo los números pares de cada línea.
   a. (6) 9 (2) 11 (4) 7 3 (8)
   b. 13 (8) (10) (6) (12) (16) 9 5
   c. (14) (16) 9 11 (12) (18) 7 (4)

3. Circle the largest number in each set.
   Encierra en un círculo el número mayor de cada serie.
   a. 26 or (32)   c. (51) or 49   e. (41) or 14
   b. 19 or (21)   d. (80) or 60   f. 67 or (76)

Write the middle consonant of each word below.
Escribe la consonante del medio de cada palabra a continuación.

| pea_n_ut | sho_v_el | whi_s_tle | ti_g_er |
| flo_w_er | wi_n_dow | un_h_appy | va_c_uum |

© Federal Education Publishing   73   Level Blue

Page 73

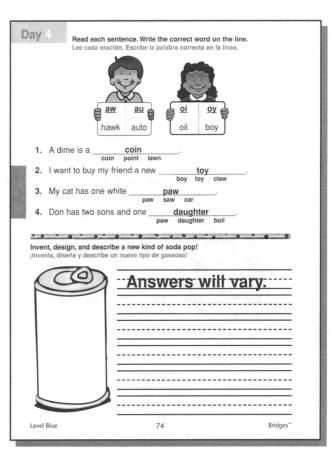

Read each sentence. Write the correct word on the line.
Lee cada oración. Escribe la palabra correcta en la línea.

| aw | au | oi | oy |
| hawk | auto | oil | boy |

1. A dime is a **coin** .
   coin point lawn
2. I want to buy my friend a new **toy** .
   boy toy claw
3. My cat has one white **paw** .
   paw saw car
4. Don has two sons and one **daughter** .
   paw daughter boil

Invent, design, and describe a new kind of soda pop!
¡Inventa, diseña y describe un nuevo tipo de gaseosa!

Answers will vary.

Level Blue   74   Bridges™

Page 74

© Federal Education Publishing   123   Level Blue

Fill in the blank space with a number to get the answer in the box.
Completa el espacio en blanco con un número para obtener la respuesta que aparece en el recuadro.

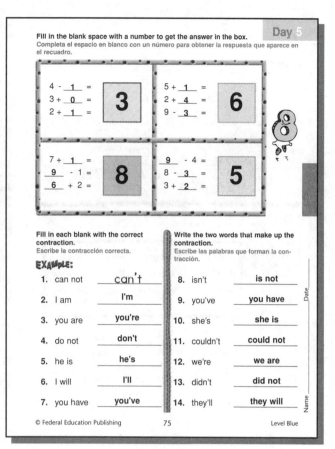

4 - _1_ =
3 + _0_ = **3**
2 + _1_ =

5 + _1_ =
2 + _4_ = **6**
9 - _3_ =

7 + _1_ =
_9_ - 1 = **8**
_6_ + 2 =

_9_ - 4 =
8 - _3_ = **5**
3 + _2_ =

Fill in each blank with the correct contraction.
Escribe la contracción correcta.

EXAMPLE:

1. can not — can't
2. I am — I'm
3. you are — you're
4. do not — don't
5. he is — he's
6. I will — I'll
7. you have — you've

Write the two words that make up the contraction.
Escribe las palabras que forman la contracción.

8. isn't — is not
9. you've — you have
10. she's — she is
11. couldn't — could not
12. we're — we are
13. didn't — did not
14. they'll — they will

© Federal Education Publishing — 75 — Level Blue

Fill in the blanks using is or are. On line 9, write a sentence using is. On line 10, write a sentence using are.
Completa los espacios en blanco con is o are. En la línea 9, escribe una oración utilizando is. En la línea 10, escribe una usando are.

1. We __are__ going to town tomorrow.
2. The cows __are__ in the field.
3. This book __is__ not mine.
4. Where __is__ a box of chalk?
5. Seals __are__ fast swimmers.
6. __Is__ he going to help you?
7. It __is__ very hot outside today.
8. __Are__ you going to the circus?
9. **Answers will vary.**
10. **Answers will vary.**

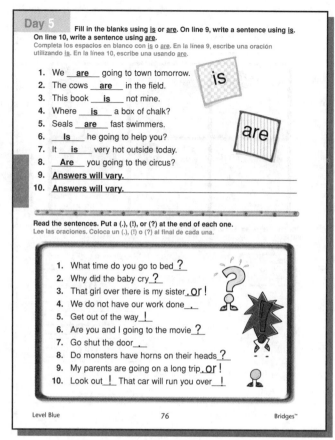

Read the sentences. Put a (.), (!), or (?) at the end of each one.
Lee las oraciones. Coloca un (.), (!) o (?) al final de cada una.

1. What time do you go to bed **?**
2. Why did the baby cry **?**
3. That girl over there is my sister **. or !**
4. We do not have our work done **.**
5. Get out of the way **!**
6. Are you and I going to the movie **?**
7. Go shut the door **.**
8. Do monsters have horns on their heads **?**
9. My parents are going on a long trip **. or !**
10. Look out **!** That car will run you over **!**

Level Blue — 76 — Bridges™

Subtract.
Resta.

A.
15	14	16	17	13
-4	-2	-8	-3	-4
11	12	8	14	9

B.
10	18	13	11	16
-4	-7	-6	-9	-5
6	11	7	2	11

C.
17	12	10	18	19
-8	-5	-1	-4	-9
9	7	9	14	10

Synonyms are words that have the same or nearly the same meaning. Find a synonym in the train for each of the words below. Write the word on the line.
Encuentra en el tren un sinónimo para cada palabra que aparece más abajo. Escribe la palabra en el espacio en blanco.

train cars: happy big ill start | easy close scared large | tidy copy quick funny

begin	**start**	afraid	**scared**	trace	**copy**
sick	**ill**	shut	**close**	fast	**quick**
glad	**happy**	simple	**easy**	silly	**funny**
large	**big**	big	**large**	neat	**tidy**

© Federal Education Publishing — 77 — Level Blue

Unscramble the scrambled word in each sentence and write it correctly.
Ordena la palabra desordenada de cada oración y escríbela correctamente.

1. A brzea is an animal in the zoo. — zebra
2. The robin has nowlf away. — flown
3. We mixed flour and eggs in a owlb. — bowl
4. Button your button and zip your rpzipe. — zipper
5. A lot of leppeo were at the game. — people
6. We met our new teacher yatdo. — today
7. My old oessh do not fit my feet. — shoes
8. We made a list of ngtihs to get. — things
9. Jim got irtyd when he fell in the mud. — dirty
10. eSktri three and you're out. — Strike

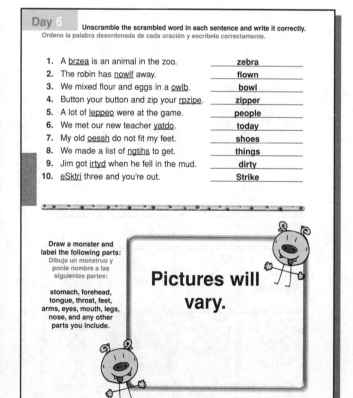

Draw a monster and label the following parts:
Dibuja un monstruo y ponle nombre a las siguientes partes:

stomach, forehead, tongue, throat, feet, arms, eyes, mouth, legs, nose, and any other parts you include.

Pictures will vary.

Level Blue — 78 — Bridges™

Level Blue — 124 — Bridges™

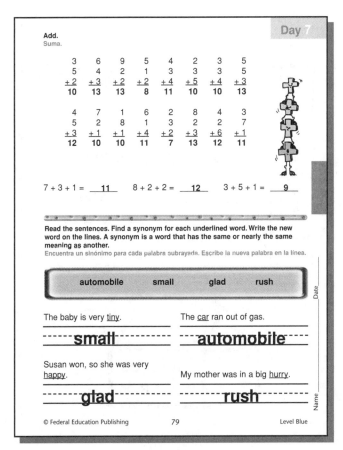

Add.
Suma.

3	6	9	5	4	2	3	5
5	4	2	1	3	3	3	5
+2	+3	+2	+2	+4	+5	+4	+3
10	13	13	8	11	10	10	13

4	7	1	6	2	8	4	3
5	2	8	1	3	2	2	7
+3	+1	+1	+4	+2	+3	+6	+1
12	10	10	11	7	13	12	11

7 + 3 + 1 = __11__   8 + 2 + 2 = __12__   3 + 5 + 1 = __9__

Read the sentences. Find a synonym for each underlined word. Write the new word on the lines. A synonym is a word that has the same or nearly the same meaning as another.
Encuentra un sinónimo para cada palabra subrayada. Escribe la nueva palabra en la línea.

automobile	small	glad	rush

The baby is very <u>tiny</u>.

small

The <u>car</u> ran out of gas.

automobile

Susan won, so she was very <u>happy</u>.

glad

My mother was in a big <u>hurry</u>.

rush

© Federal Education Publishing   79   Level Blue

Page 79

Day 7

Make an X by the answers to the questions.
Coloca una X delante de las respuestas a las preguntas.

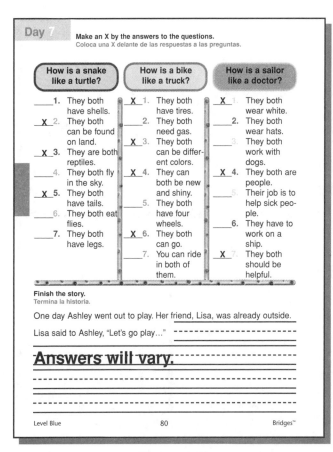

How is a snake like a turtle?
- ____ 1. They both have shells.
- _X_ 2. They both can be found on land.
- _X_ 3. They are both reptiles.
- ____ 4. They both fly in the sky.
- _X_ 5. They both have tails.
- ____ 6. They both eat flies.
- ____ 7. They both have legs.

How is a bike like a truck?
- _X_ 1. They both have tires.
- ____ 2. They both need gas.
- _X_ 3. They both can be different colors.
- _X_ 4. They can both be new and shiny.
- ____ 5. They both have four wheels.
- _X_ 6. They both can go.
- ____ 7. You can ride in both of them.

How is a sailor like a doctor?
- _X_ 1. They both wear white.
- ____ 2. They both wear hats.
- ____ 3. They both work with dogs.
- _X_ 4. They both are people.
- ____ 5. Their job is to help sick people.
- ____ 6. They have to work on a ship.
- _X_ 7. They both should be helpful.

Finish the story.
Termina la historia.

One day Ashley went out to play. Her friend, Lisa, was already outside.

Lisa said to Ashley, "Let's go play…"

Answers will vary.

Level Blue   80   Bridges™

Page 80

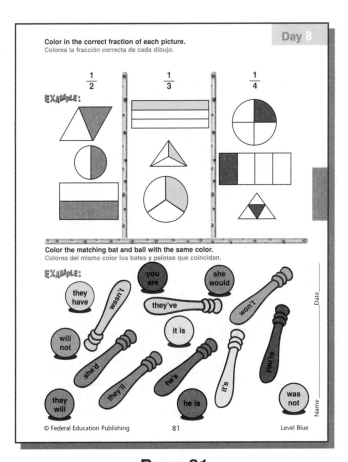

Color in the correct fraction of each picture.
Colorea la fracción correcta de cada dibujo.

$\frac{1}{2}$ $\frac{1}{3}$ $\frac{1}{4}$

EXAMPLE:

Color the matching bat and ball with the same color.
Colorea del mismo color los bates y pelotas que coincidan.

EXAMPLE:

they have · wasn't · you are · she would · they've · won't · will not · it is · she'd · they'll · he's · it's · you're · they will · he is · was not

© Federal Education Publishing   81   Level Blue

Page 81

Day 8

Make up five funny sentences using one word from each column on the hot-air balloon. Do not use any of the words more than once.
Inventa cinco oraciones divertidas usando una palabra de cada columna del globo. Usa cada palabra solamente una vez.

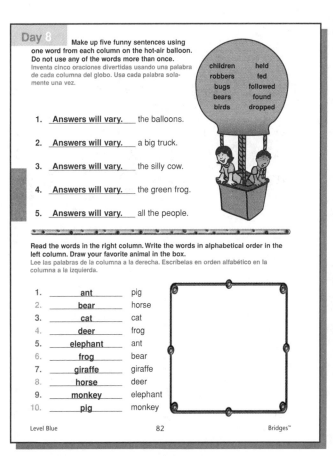

children	held
robbers	fed
bugs	followed
bears	found
birds	dropped

1. __Answers will vary.__ the balloons.
2. __Answers will vary.__ a big truck.
3. __Answers will vary.__ the silly cow.
4. __Answers will vary.__ the green frog.
5. __Answers will vary.__ all the people.

Read the words in the right column. Write the words in alphabetical order in the left column. Draw your favorite animal in the box.
Lee las palabras de la columna a la derecha. Escríbelas en orden alfabético en la columna a la izquierda.

#	(left column)	(right column)
1.	ant	pig
2.	bear	horse
3.	cat	cat
4.	deer	frog
5.	elephant	ant
6.	frog	bear
7.	giraffe	giraffe
8.	horse	deer
9.	monkey	elephant
10.	pig	monkey

Level Blue   82   Bridges™

Page 82

Page 83

Add or subtract.
Suma o resta.

11	18	3	10	17	13	18	19
+7	+1	+7	-3	-2	+6	-6	-7
18	**19**	**10**	**7**	**15**	**19**	**12**	**12**

33	64	5	2	12	14	27	16
+5	-3	+3	+4	-7	-11	-3	-8
38	**61**	**8**	**6**	**5**	**3**	**24**	**8**

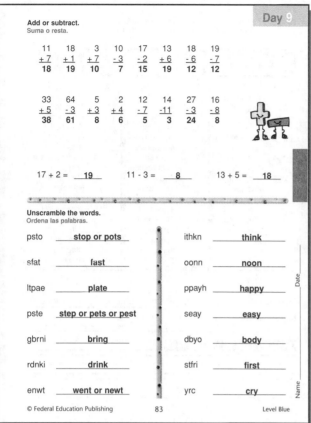

17 + 2 = __19__   11 - 3 = __8__   13 + 5 = __18__

Unscramble the words.
Ordena las palabras.

psto	__stop or pots__		ithkn	__think__
sfat	__fast__		oonn	__noon__
ltpae	__plate__		ppayh	__happy__
pste	__step or pets or pest__		seay	__easy__
gbrni	__bring__		dbyo	__body__
rdnki	__drink__		stfri	__first__
enwt	__went or newt__		yrc	__cry__

Date

Name

© Federal Education Publishing   83   Level Blue

Page 84

Read the words aloud; then write them in alphabetical order.
Lee las palabras en voz alta y luego escríbelas en orden alfabético.

rabbit
snake
lion
dog
fish
dish
make
candy
puppy
vase

1. candy
2. dish
3. dog
4. fish
5. lion
6. make
7. puppy
8. rabbit
9. snake
10. vase

Dairy Designs. A dairy company has asked you to create a design for a milk carton. Create and color an original milk carton design for the company.
Crea un diseño original de un envase de cartón para la leche.

Pictures will vary.

Level Blue   84   Bridges™

Page 85

Color the coins that match the given amount.
Colorea las monedas que correspondan a la cantidad dada.

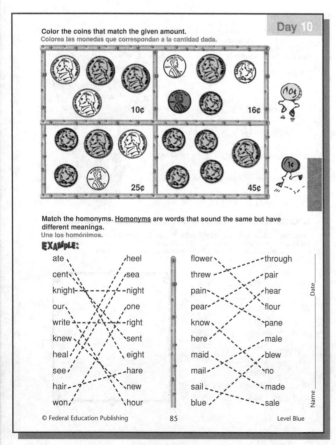

10¢   16¢

25¢   45¢

Match the homonyms. <u>Homonyms</u> are words that sound the same but have different meanings.
Une los homónimos.

EXAMPLE:

ate — heel
cent — sea
knight — night
our — one
write — right
knew — sent
heal — eight
see — hare
hair — new
won — hour

flower — through
threw — pair
pain — hear
pear — flour
know — pane
here — male
maid — blew
mail — no
sail — made
blue — sale

Date

Name

© Federal Education Publishing   85   Level Blue

Page 86

Read these silly sentences! Put a 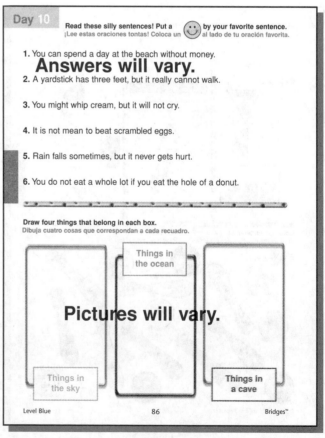 by your favorite sentence.
¡Lee estas oraciones tontas! Coloca un 😊 al lado de tu oración favorita.

1. You can spend a day at the beach without money.

Answers will vary.

2. A yardstick has three feet, but it really cannot walk.

3. You might whip cream, but it will not cry.

4. It is not mean to beat scrambled eggs.

5. Rain falls sometimes, but it never gets hurt.

6. You do not eat a whole lot if you eat the hole of a donut.

Draw four things that belong in each box.
Dibuja cuatro cosas que correspondan a cada recuadro.

Things in the sky   Things in the ocean   Things in a cave

Pictures will vary.

Level Blue   86   Bridges™

Page 87

Add or subtract.
Suma o resta.

1.
10	18	7	7	8	6	9	4	9
-4	-14	-3	+5	+2	-4	-4	+7	+2
6	4	4	12	10	2	5	11	11

2.
11	11	10	9	8	9	7	10	11
-1	+8	-8	+8	+2	+1	-5	-3	-7
10	19	2	17	10	10	2	7	4

8 + 6 = __14__   9 + 3 = __12__   4 + 9 = __13__

Antonyms. Match the words with opposite meanings.
Une las palabras con el significado opuesto.

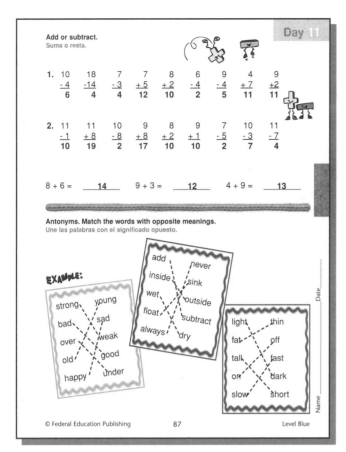

EXAMPLE:

strong — young
bad — sad
over — weak
old — good
happy — under

add — never
inside — sink
wet — outside
float — subtract
always — dry

light — thin
fat — off
tall — fast
on — dark
slow — short

© Federal Education Publishing   87   Level Blue

Page 87

Page 88

Read each sentence. Do what it tells you to do. Then put a ✔ in the box to show that you have finished that step.
Haz lo que cada oración te diga que hagas. Coloca un ✔ en el recuadro luego de que lo hayas hecho.

Let's get ready for lunch.

☐ Draw a plate on the place mat.
☐ Draw a napkin on the left side of the plate.
☐ Draw a fork on the napkin.
☐ Draw a knife and spoon on the right side of the plate.
☐ Draw a glass of purple juice above the napkin.
☐ Draw your favorite lunch.

Answers will vary.

Enjoy!

Finish this story.
Finaliza la historia.

If I could fly anywhere, I would fly to _____
because... _____

Answers will vary.

Level Blue   88   Bridges™

Page 88

Page 89

Finish each table.
Termina las tablas.

Add 10	
5	15
8	18
7	17
9	19
3	13
4	14

Add 8	
2	10
6	14
4	12
7	15
3	11
5	13

Add 6	
10	16
6	12
8	14
7	13
4	10
5	11

Circle the correctly spelled word in each row.
Encierra en un círculo la palabra escrita correctamente en cada línea.

1. ca'nt   can'nt   (can't)
2. esy   (easy)   eazy
3. crie   cri   (cry)
4. kea   (key)   kee
5. (buy)   buye   biy
6. lihg   (light)   ligte
7. allready   (already)   alredy
8. summ   som   (some)
9. sekond   secund   (second)
10. (hasn't)   has'nt   hasent

11. wonce   onse   (once)
12. pritty   preety   (pretty)
13. (carry)   carey   carrie
14. (you're)   yure   yo're
15. parte   (part)   parrt
16. (star)   stor   starr
17. funy   (funny)   funnie
18. babie   babey   (baby)
19. mabe   (maybe)   maybee
20. therde   therd   (third)

© Federal Education Publishing   89   Level Blue

Page 89

Page 90

Circle the correct answer.
Encierra en un círculo la respuesta correcta.

1. Another name for <u>boy</u> is: girl   (son)   funny
2. After seven comes: six   nine   (eight)
3. I bite with: wheel   (teeth)   arms
4. A car and truck roll on: with   whip   (wheels)
5. A farmer grows: ship   (wheat)   land
6. Your brain helps you: this   thing   (think)
7. A chair can also be a: (seat)   sound   safe
8. A rabbit has: while   whirl   (whiskers)

Do the crossword puzzle.
Haz el crucigrama.

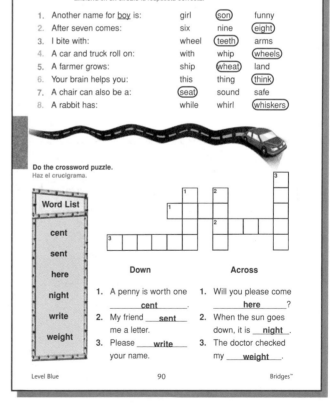

Word List
cent
sent
here
night
write
weight

Down

1. A penny is worth one ___**cent**___.
2. My friend ___**sent**___ me a letter.
3. Please ___**write**___ your name.

Across

1. Will you please come ___**here**___?
2. When the sun goes down, it is ___**night**___.
3. The doctor checked my ___**weight**___.

Level Blue   90   Bridges™

Page 90

Page 91

Make number sentences. Use only the numbers in the circles.
Forma operaciones con los números. Usa solamente los números encerrados en los círculos.

EXAMPLE:

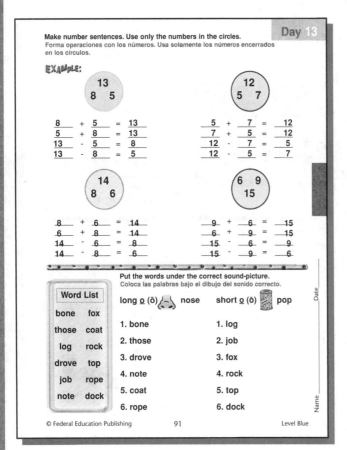

Circle 1: 13 / 8 5

$8 + 5 = 13$
$5 + 8 = 13$
$13 - 5 = 8$
$13 - 8 = 5$

Circle 2: 12 / 5 7

$5 + 7 = 12$
$7 + 5 = 12$
$12 - 7 = 5$
$12 - 5 = 7$

Circle 3: 14 / 8 6

$8 + 6 = 14$
$6 + 8 = 14$
$14 - 6 = 8$
$14 - 8 = 6$

Circle 4: 6 9 / 15

$9 + 6 = 15$
$6 + 9 = 15$
$15 - 6 = 9$
$15 - 9 = 6$

Put the words under the correct sound-picture.
Coloca las palabras bajo el dibujo del sonido correcto.

Word List

bone fox
those coat
log rock
drove top
job rope
note dock

long o (ō) nose

1. bone
2. those
3. drove
4. note
5. coat
6. rope

short o (ŏ) pop

1. log
2. job
3. fox
4. rock
5. top
6. dock

Date ___
Name ___

© Federal Education Publishing   91   Level Blue

Page 92

Circle and write the action verb in each sentence.
Encierra en un círculo y escribe el verbo activo de cada oración.

EXAMPLE:

1. The chicken (ran) away. _ran_
2. Judy (cut) her finger with the knife. cut
3. A kangaroo can (hop) very fast. hop
4. I like to (swim) in our pool. swim
5. Ted and Sid will (chop) some wood. chop
6. That kitten likes to (climb) trees. climb
7. We will (eat) dinner at six o'clock. eat
8. The baby was (yawning) yawning
9. The car (crashed) into a tree. crashed
10. Please (peel) this orange for me. peel

Draw a face beside each statement that tells how it makes you feel.
Al lado de cada oración, dibuja una cara que muestre como te hace sentir.

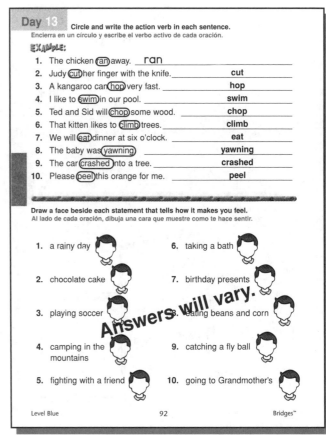

1. a rainy day
2. chocolate cake
3. playing soccer
4. camping in the mountains
5. fighting with a friend
6. taking a bath
7. birthday presents
8. eating beans and corn
9. catching a fly ball
10. going to Grandmother's

Answers will vary.

Level Blue   92   Bridges™

Page 93

Add.
Suma.

1.
3	3	6	2	4	5	7	3
2	4	1	2	3	4	1	5
+1	+2	+2	+3	+3	+6	+2	+4
6	9	9	7	10	15	10	12

2.
1	6	7	4	5	4	8	4
3	3	2	5	2	4	1	6
+2	+1	+1	+2	+3	+1	+2	+3
6	10	10	11	10	9	11	13

Write soft c words under pencil. Write hard c words under candy.
Escribe palabras con c suave bajo pencil. Escribe palabras con c fuerte bajo candy.

grocery cattle cement corn price
cake cellar crib grace cow

pencil

1. grocery
2. cellar
3. cement
4. grace
5. price

candy

1. cake
2. cattle
3. crib
4. corn
5. cow

Date ___
Name ___

© Federal Education Publishing   93   Level Blue

Page 94

Unscramble the sentences. Write the words in the correct order.
Ordena las oraciones. Escribe las palabras en el orden correcto.

1. sun shine will today The.

The sun will shine today.

2. mile today I a walked.

I walked a mile today.

3. house We painted our.

We painted our house.

4. Mother knit will I something for.

I will knit something for Mother.

Write a letter. Ask someone to a silly picnic.
Escribe una carta para invitar a alguien a un pic-nic absurdo.

Start your letter with "Dear _____,"
End your letter with "Yours truly, _____."

Answers will vary.

Level Blue   94   Bridges™

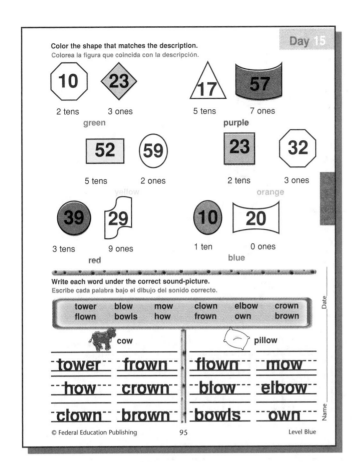

Page 95

Color the shape that matches the description.
Colorea la figura que coincida con la descripción.

10 — 2 tens — green
23 — 3 ones
17 — 5 tens
57 — 7 ones — purple

52 — 5 tens
59 — 2 ones — yellow
23 — 2 tens
32 — 3 ones — orange

39 — 3 tens
29 — 9 ones — red
10 — 1 ten
20 — 0 ones — blue

Write each word under the correct sound-picture.
Escribe cada palabra bajo el dibujo del sonido correcto.

| tower | blow | mow | clown | elbow | crown |
| flown | bowls | how | frown | own | brown |

cow

pillow

tower — frown — flown — mow

how — crown — blow — elbow

clown — brown — bowls — own

Page 96

Draw a line to the right word.
Dibuja una línea hasta la palabra correcta.

EXAMPLE:
1. Something near you is
2. Something that tells time is a
3. A time of day is
4. A crow is a kind of
5. A place where fish live is an
6. Pork is a kind of
7. Chicks, ducklings, and fawns are kinds of
8. A shop is a kind of
9. To hit something is to
10. To look in someone else's things is to

clock
bird
babies
snoop
close
dusk
aquarium
strike
store
meat

Write as many words as you can that describe…
Escribe todas las palabras que puedas para describir estas cosas.

ice cream

watermelon

Answers will vary.

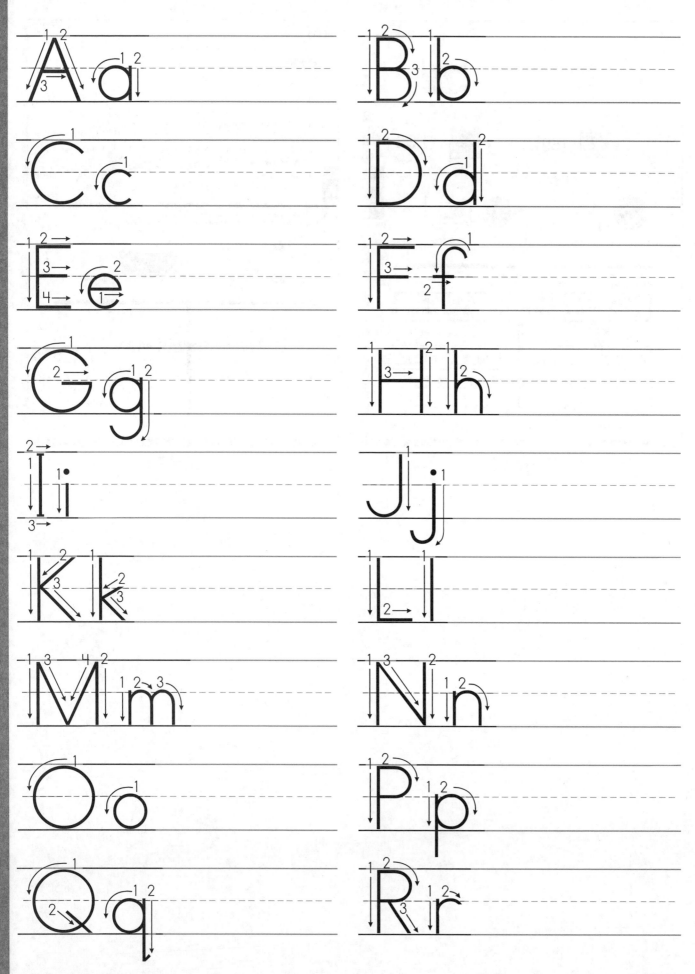

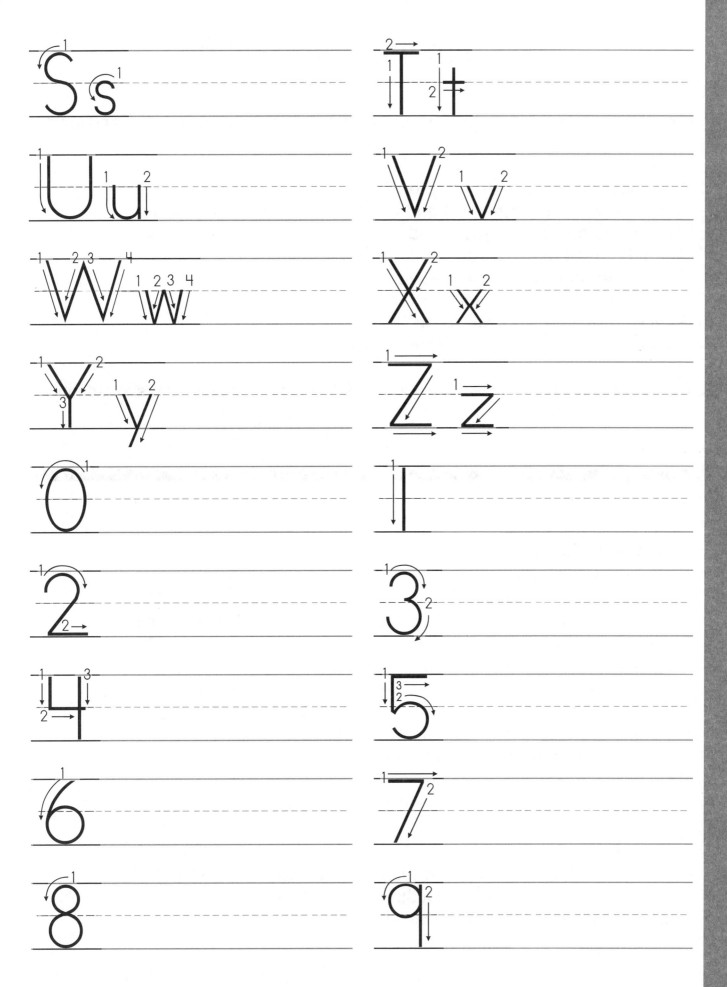

Addition and Subtraction

Developing math skills can be a challenging experience for both parent and child.

- **Have a positive attitude.**
- **Relax and enjoy the learning process.**
- **Keep the learning time short and fun. You will get better results.**
- **Review the cards with your child.**
- **Read the front of the card.**
- **Check your answer on the reverse side.**
- **Separate those he/she does not know.**
- **Review those he/she does know.**
- **Gradually work through the other cards.**

These steps will help build your child's confidence with addition and subtraction. Enjoy the rewards!

"Teacher, Teacher"

Three or more players.
Each player takes a turn as "Teacher."
The Teacher mixes up the flashcards and holds one card up at a time.
First player to yell out "Teacher, Teacher,"
will have the first chance to give the answer.
If his/her answer is right, he/she receives 5 points.
If his/her answer is wrong, he/she will not receive any points.
Move on to the next person until someone answers correctly.
The next round someone else is teacher.
Repeat each round.
Reward the different levels: everyone wins!

Time Challenge

Follow the directions for "Teacher, Teacher" and add a time to it.
Increase the point system to meet the Time Challenge.
Reward the different levels: everyone wins!

0 + 0	2 + 0	4 + 0	5 + 0
3	2	1	0
8 + 0	0 + 1	1 + 1	2 + 1
7	6	5	4
5 + 1	7 + 1	9 + 1	2 + 2
1	0	9	8

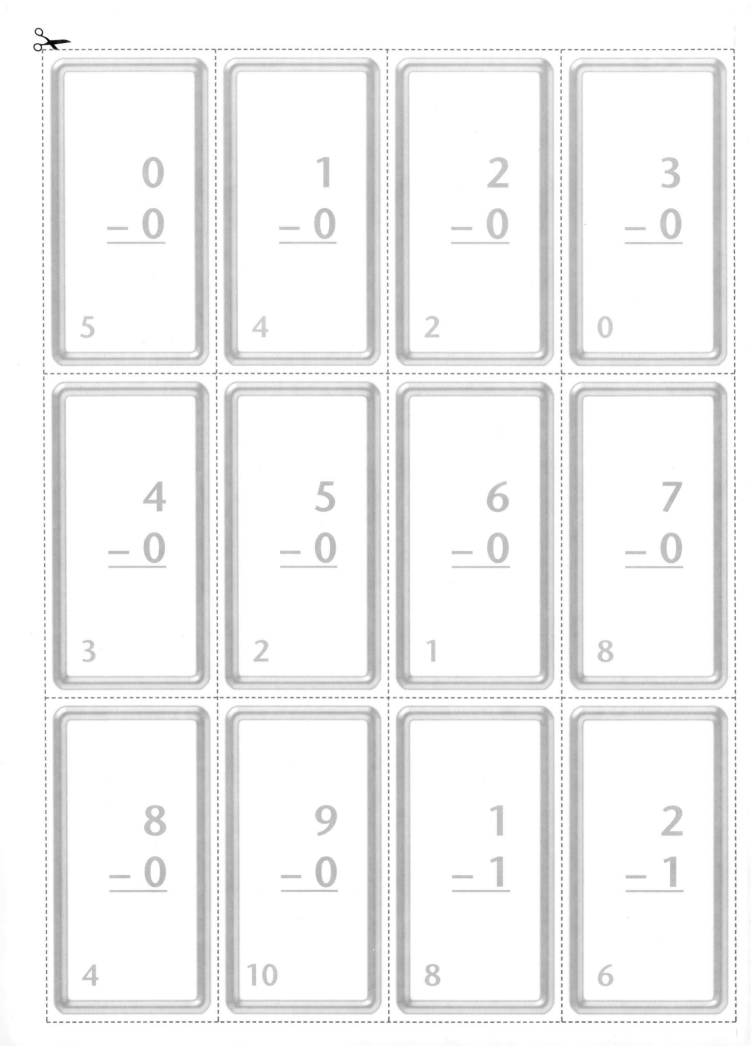

0 − 0 5	1 − 0 4	2 − 0 2	3 − 0 0
4 − 0 3	5 − 0 2	6 − 0 1	7 − 0 8
8 − 0 4	9 − 0 10	1 − 1 8	2 − 1 6

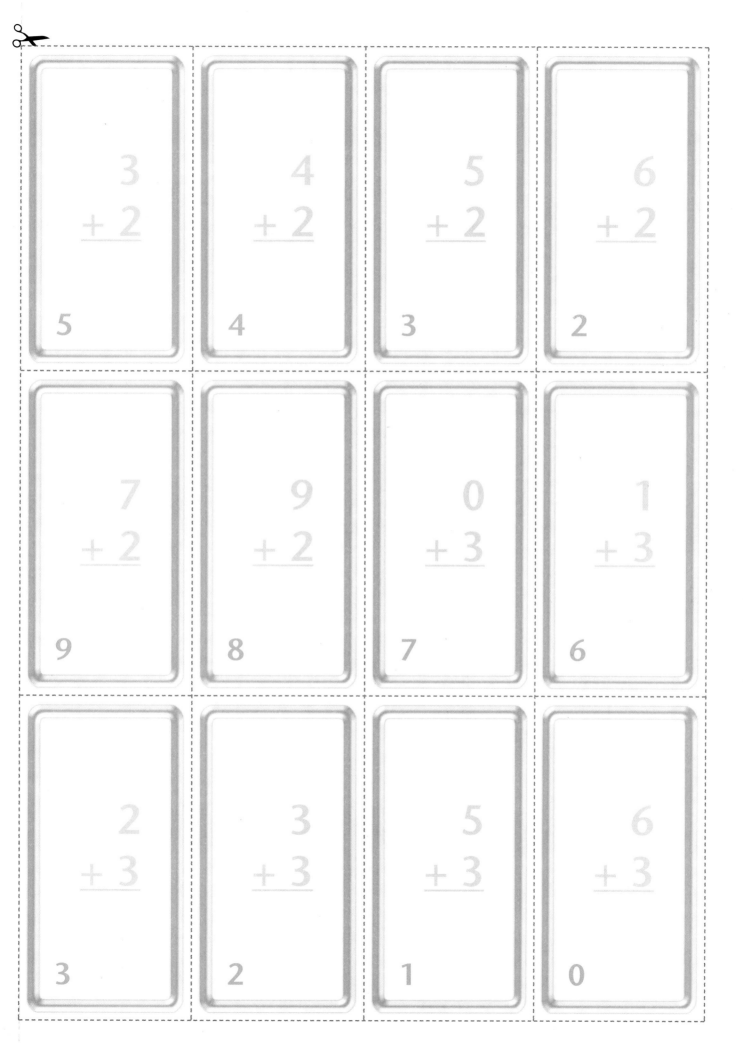

3 + 2 5	4 + 2 4	5 + 2 3	6 + 2 2
7 + 2 9	9 + 2 8	0 + 3 7	1 + 3 6
2 + 3 3	3 + 3 2	5 + 3 1	6 + 3 0

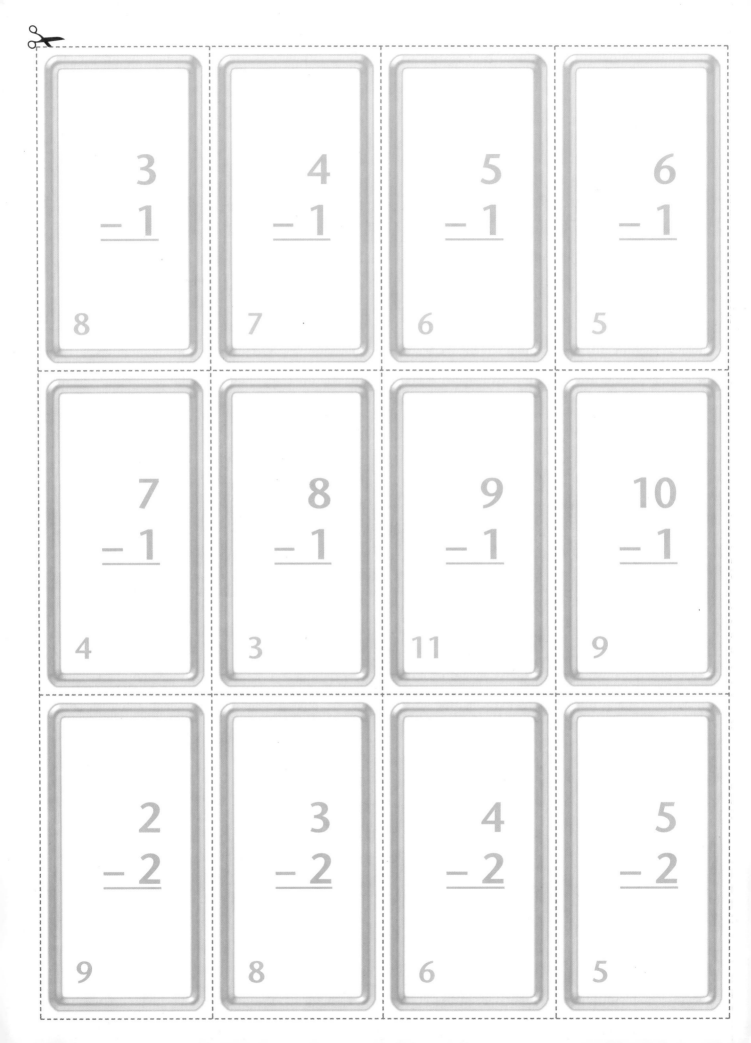

3 − 1	4 − 1	5 − 1	6 − 1
8	7	6	5
7 − 1	8 − 1	9 − 1	10 − 1
4	3	11	9
2 − 2	3 − 2	4 − 2	5 − 2
9	8	6	5

$\begin{array}{r}8\\+\,3\\\hline\end{array}$	$\begin{array}{r}9\\+\,3\\\hline\end{array}$	$\begin{array}{r}1\\+\,4\\\hline\end{array}$	$\begin{array}{r}3\\+\,4\\\hline\end{array}$
7	6	5	4
$\begin{array}{r}4\\+\,4\\\hline\end{array}$	$\begin{array}{r}5\\+\,4\\\hline\end{array}$	$\begin{array}{r}7\\+\,4\\\hline\end{array}$	$\begin{array}{r}8\\+\,4\\\hline\end{array}$
1	0	9	8
$\begin{array}{r}9\\+\,4\\\hline\end{array}$	$\begin{array}{r}2\\+\,5\\\hline\end{array}$	$\begin{array}{r}3\\+\,5\\\hline\end{array}$	$\begin{array}{r}5\\+\,5\\\hline\end{array}$
5	4	3	2

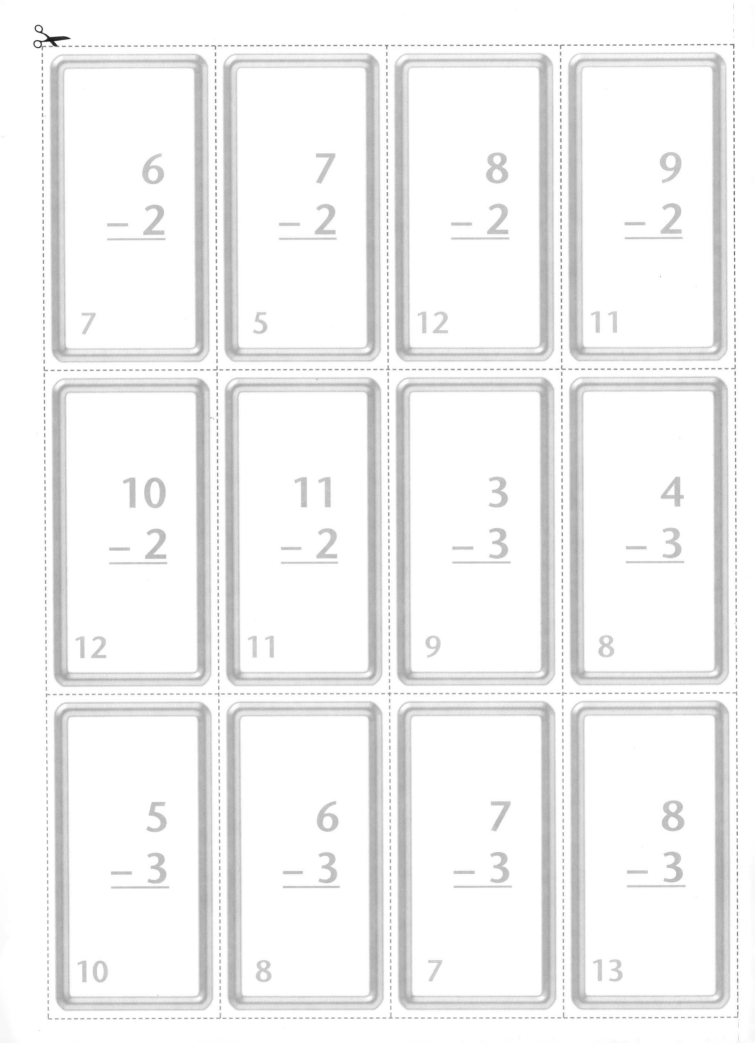

6 − 2	7 − 2	8 − 2	9 − 2
7	5	12	11
10 − 2	11 − 2	3 − 3	4 − 3
12	11	9	8
5 − 3	6 − 3	7 − 3	8 − 3
10	8	7	13

✂

7 $+\,5$	8 $+\,5$	9 $+\,5$	1 $+\,6$
9	8	7	6
2 $+\,6$	4 $+\,6$	5 $+\,6$	6 $+\,6$
3	2	1	0
7 $+\,6$	8 $+\,6$	0 $+\,7$	1 $+\,7$
7	6	5	4

9 − 3	10 − 3	11 − 3	12 − 3
7	14	13	12
4 − 4	5 − 4	6 − 4	7 − 4
12	11	10	8
8 − 4	9 − 4	10 − 4	11 − 4
8	7	14	13

✂

2 + 7 1	3 + 7 0	4 + 7 9	5 + 7 8
7 + 7 5	8 + 7 4	1 + 8 3	2 + 8 2
3 + 8 9	5 + 8 8	6 + 8 7	8 + 8 6

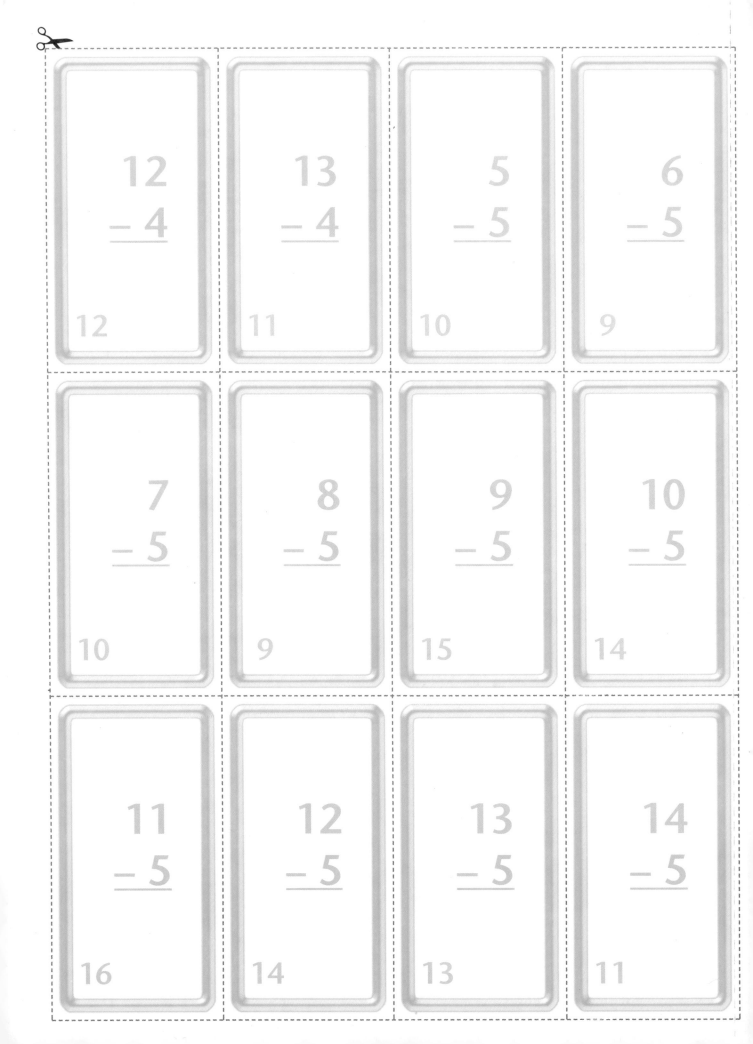

12 − 4 12	13 − 4 11	5 − 5 10	6 − 5 9
7 − 5 10	8 − 5 9	9 − 5 15	10 − 5 14
11 − 5 16	12 − 5 14	13 − 5 13	14 − 5 11

✂

$\begin{array}{r} 9 \\ +8 \\ \hline \end{array}$	$\begin{array}{r} 0 \\ +9 \\ \hline \end{array}$	$\begin{array}{r} 2 \\ +9 \\ \hline \end{array}$	$\begin{array}{r} 4 \\ +9 \\ \hline \end{array}$
7	6	5	4
$\begin{array}{r} 6 \\ +9 \\ \hline \end{array}$	$\begin{array}{r} 7 \\ +9 \\ \hline \end{array}$	$\begin{array}{r} 8 \\ +9 \\ \hline \end{array}$	$\begin{array}{r} 9 \\ +9 \\ \hline \end{array}$
1	0	9	8
$\begin{array}{r} 6 \\ -6 \\ \hline \end{array}$	$\begin{array}{r} 7 \\ -6 \\ \hline \end{array}$	$\begin{array}{r} 8 \\ -6 \\ \hline \end{array}$	$\begin{array}{r} 9 \\ -6 \\ \hline \end{array}$
5	4	3	2

10 − 6	11 − 6	12 − 6	13 − 6
13	11	9	17
14 − 6	15 − 6	7 − 7	8 − 7
18	17	16	15
9 − 7	10 − 7	11 − 7	12 − 7
3	2	1	0

13 − 7	14 − 7	15 − 7	16 − 7
1	0	9	8
8 − 8	9 − 8	10 − 8	11 − 8
5	4	3	2
12 − 8	13 − 8	14 − 8	15 − 8
9	8	7	6

16 − 8	17 − 8	9 − 9	10 − 9
9	8	7	6
11 − 9	12 − 9	13 − 9	14 − 9
3	2	1	0
15 − 9	16 − 9	17 − 9	18 − 9
7	6	5	4

Certificate of Completion

(Certificado de Cumplimiento)

Awarded to
(Otorgado a)

for the completion of *Bridges*
(por completar *Bridges*)

Teacher's Signature
(Firma del Maestro)

Parent's Signature
(Firma del Padre)

bridges